HORSES TALK: IT PAYS TO LISTEN

The Paddock and Post Parade

by
Trillis Parker

For the serious Horse Player: What others won't tell you—about Paddock and Post Parade Inspection, signposts to longshots, and much more. Featuring detailed descriptions, drawings and photos on what you need to know about the Thoroughbred Race Horse.

"Library of Congress Catalog Card Number:" 88-93037
ISBN 0-915700-07-7

1st Printing December 1986
2nd Printing March 1987
3rd Printing Spring 1988
Revised Printing January 1989

PRINTED IN THE UNITED STATES OF AMERICA

Cover Artwork: Patrick (Dino) Derouineau
Cover Design: Robert G. Cain
Photography: Steve Stidham Photography
Additional Photos: Curt Carlson, Millard Richards.

Published by: PARKER PRODUCTIONS, INC.

Distributed by: LIBERTY PUBLISHING COMPANY, INC.
440 S. Federal Highway
Deerfield Beach, FL 33441

Illustrations on pages 19, 21, 22, 24–28 reprinted by permission of the Ontario Jockey Club and the Canadian Thoroughbred Horse Society. A special Thanks to them both.

To dedicated Handicappers, full or part time—

In appreciation of their many hours devoted to Thoroughbred Handicapping,
I share with them my knowledge.

Trillis Parker

PARKER PRODUCTIONS, INC.

Horses Talk Series: Plus Much More

5118 Placentia Parkway
Las Vegas, NV 89118

CONTENTS

INTRODUCTION

This book takes the reader through the learning process of someone who has developed expertise in the only way possible—through time, energy, and constant alertness to new discoveries.

I am totally convinced that in today's racing, anywhere in the country, the strongest (and possibly ONLY) WINNING EDGE in achieving parimutuel profits is through the skills the reader can obtain from this book, and applying its content to the race track battlefield.

Before you begin reading "Horses Talk: It Pays To Listen," I would put forth three important NOTES.

I am one of many horse players that has read most of what goes under the heading of "racing literature." In most cases, one works through several hundred pages of bromides for the few "golden nuggets" of valuable information that are hopefully derived from the time spent in the reading.

NOTE #1—you are about to read the most valuable pages in print. The bulk of it should be read repeatedly, until the material is literally burned into memory. In this book, the reader will find a Gold Mine, rather than a few pebble-sized "nuggets."

NOTE #2—it would be very easy for a reader, particularly the first time through, to be overwhelmed, to come away thinking "this is fantastic, but I can't do it, this is for the scattered few with a special ability."

Not true. In terms of perception, few could exceed my limitations—which range from bad eyesight to difficulty in concentration at a race track, poor organization to "brains but no common sense." (In my book and later writings, I have focused on much that was directed to solving personal weaknesses, and assisting those with similar characteristics.)

I cannot describe the thrill of cashing boxcar payoffs, as gradually and increasingly the contents of this book are mastered. There are a few things (such as horses with "stickers" on a fast track) that my eyes are not good enough to catch. So if Trillis is not with me, I would take along someone with sharper eyesight and "team play."

DO NOT be intimidated by the content of this book. There is NOTHING herein that you cannot learn, master, and apply—your only need is some time and practice. For a few, it takes a little longer—but letters in our files from seminar students and our publication subscribers attest to both the thrill and the profit when it all "comes together."

NOTE #3—in betting into this magnificent EDGE, as in any other focus, maximum profits depend on the effectiveness of Money Management. In our case, both Trillis and I could be described as "timid" bettors. But over the years, I have learned that MOST horse players become intimidated by Tote Board odds. They bet less, not more, as odds increase. And some find it nearly impossible to bet a horse that is above 10–1.

Applying the content of this book will give the horse player the highest average winning payoff that will ever be found in any specific handicapping approach. It is VITAL to lose these inhibitions. In the final Chapter, I will intrude upon Trillis's fine work to outline some wagering criteria—my personal appraisal of "when and how to bet" in terms of application of this specialized approach to Thoroughbred handicapping and parimutuel wagering.

I am extremely proud of Trillis, her book and all that preceded it; but particularly for her willingness and desire to share this EDGE with all who are willing to take a little time, open their minds, and benefit from what is offered.

Trillis Parker has also introduced two videos for 1989, designed to visually elaborate on "Horses Talk: "It Pays To Listen." Video #1, "Horses Talk: Where It Begins—The Early Years" provides two rare insights accessible to few horse players that are not owners or breeders.

The "Body Signs" begin when the horse is still at mother's side. This is where attitude and competitive nature are initially formed. At the yearling sale, conformation (good and bad) is examined, along with inferences to performance.

Few winning (and betting) trainers are willing to "go public" with what they do, and why. Trillis further struck gold for the horse player/viewer in connecting with a trainer who "cares" about fans, and what is good for racing.

Through "The Early Years," the viewer will learn to recognize every piece of equipment used on a Thoroughbred, the reasons for each and Handicapping implications. The "slide bit," and the "cage bit" infer almost automatic bets when viewed in the paddock. The trainer covers everything that will happen to the Thoroughbred from yearling sale acquisition to "race ready" status.

Among Thoroughbreds illustrating the "positive body signs," footage is included of ALYSHEBA, SNOW CHIEF, FERDINAND, SKYWALKER, and others—overall content made possible by the Bay Meadows Racing Association, Santa Anita, and Hollywood Park.

Video #2, "Horses Talk: The Paddock and Post Parade" concentrates on the race day vantage points. The viewer is bombarded with visual examples of key body signs. This is where 20–1 to 50–1 horses can be recognized and backed. The "paddock player" must be patient; plays are not "high volume." But, oh what an average payoff!

I highly recommend to all purchasing this book, and/or the videos, to drop a line to Trillis Parker. She keeps a personal and private mailing list, from time to time sending out letters on new discoveries. She is one of the few who holds nothing back, committed to on-going teaching.

—James N. Selvidge

ACKNOWLEDGEMENTS

If it were not for the kind urging, literary intelligence and financial backing of my better half, James N. Selvidge, I would not be attempting this publication. If not for his daily escort to the track, and now the race books, I would not have been able to compile the information you are about to read.

A special thanks to the late Dr. Young for his interest in and support of my hobby of Thoroughbred racing. Never once did he complain if I had my head in a *Daily Racing Form* while at work. Thanks, Doc, I know you are watching over us and would approve.

Others whom I thank for their generous assistance and support are Dorothy Henderson, Bonnie Ledbetter, Martie Ludtke, Jerome Molenda, and Bonnie Valente.

Thank you Mike Molenda for your legal and business acumen. Your street skills are very much appreciated.

Many thanks to Larry Hoffman for his continued assistance with track variants.

I am deeply grateful to four very special people, George, Rita and Curt Carlson, and Millard Richards. They donated their time and effort in shooting some of the hard to get pictures for this book. My sincere thanks to you all.

I want to express my deepest appreciation and love to my family for putting up with me: my Mother, Vida Evans; my Sons, Ed and Marc Parker; and my Cousin, Norma Jean Nelson Knutzen and her beloved Silver.

I.
THE PROCESS OF LEARNING

THE PROCESS OF LEARNING

Attending the races for the very first time was for me, I'm sure, much like many others: "Beginner's Luck."

Friends had invited me to join them for the day at a track very near to my residence. After inquiring of the expenses that would be encountered, I decided I could spare $10.00 for the day's entertainment. My budget was extremely tight for I was a single parent raising two sons on my own. I was so excited just thinking that I was finally going to the races.

It was such a gorgeous day. People everywhere eating, drinking and yes, even dancing. It was a Saturday; a band played music before the actual races started and many were taking advantage of it.

We found some seats in the bar located very close to the finish line. I was so confused at first. I asked, "What are the numbers on the monitors?" After being acquainted with the tote board, the program, the *Daily Racing Form,* and the betting windows, my mind was pretty much scrambled and my taste buds decided they were thirsty. With a couple of sips of my usual diet soda, I settled down and tried to make my selection for the first race. While listening to my friends discuss the races, I had overheard them state that horses sired by COLD COMMAND or STRONG RULER were running well at this track. "Sired, what does sired mean?" I was so embarrassed asking so many questions.

With a brief explanation, I glanced through the first race and couldn't see either one of the sires mentioned, so I didn't bet. I walked out, close to the finish line, to watch the race. "And there they go"—the race was on—what was happening?—everyone was standing and screaming. I couldn't hear the announcer—who was in front?—what was going on? Then, all of a sudden, I could see a mass of thundering hooves racing towards the finish line—and then it was over.

The second race was about to go off and I noticed that one of the horses was sired by COLD COMMAND, so I decided to bet on it. "How do I bet?", I asked the window teller. "What's the number of the horse you want to bet on lady?" "Number six," I replied. "How much do you want to bet?" "The smallest I can," I said. "O.K. two dollars. Do you want it to win, place, or show?" "Oh, I'll bet it to show"—seemed logical at the time for, then, I had three chances to collect. "O.K. lady, here's your ticket."

I decided then to watch the race on the TV monitor, knowing I could view the race better. "And there they go"—the race was on. Where's the horse I bet on? I couldn't see him—oh gosh there he is—come on boy, "GO! GO! GO!" All of a sudden I was jumping up and down, screaming just like everyone else. My heart was pounding and my hands were wet with perspiration—my horse was in front—"He won!"—"He won!"—how wonderfully exciting. "Did you bet him?" my friends asked. "Yes, I bet him to show"—"Should have bet him to win," they replied, "he's going to pay a lot of money." "Oh well, at least I get to cash a ticket." Cashing my winning tickets was the easiest part of the day.

The third race was just as exciting, for there was a horse running sired by STRONG RULER. This time I bet to win, and sure enough, it did. This was so easy, I thought. If this is all you have to do I should come more often.

The fourth and fifth races had me moving—to the betting windows and then to the cashiers cage. What a day! It was wonderful. By this time my thirst had developed again, and my stomach was growling. I grabbed another soda and a hot dog, and downed them quickly for the sixth race was a field of two year olds and I was informed we were going to the paddock to look at them. "The paddock! where and what is that?" I knew I had just about drowned my friends with questions, but I just had to ask. Off we went.

At the paddock we squeezed ourselves between all the people up close to the railing. I was beginning to get a little nervous, for my experience up close to horses hadn't been the best. Most of the horses were quite mannerly—except for one. As this horse approached the area in the paddock where I was standing, he became more and more unruly, whirling and twirling all over the place. The fellow that was trying to control the horse had an awful time. All of a sudden, right in front of me, the horse reared up—I squealed and turned quickly to get out of the way. As I turned I accidentally hit the person behind me, who was holding a cold drink of some kind, and you can imagine what happened to that. I really didn't care, though, for all I wanted to do was get away from there as quickly as possible.

I was frantic—I don't know who was more frightened, the horse or me. As I glanced back to see if I had gotten to a safe place, I noticed that the horse had calmed down and everyone was still mingled close to the railing. After collecting my composure it dawned on me there was absolutely no way the horse could have hurt me. Everyone else knew that at the time, but I sure didn't. All I could see was a pair of big hooves over me, heading in my direction. My friends finally caught up with me, and were concerned as to why I left so abruptly. I explained, and elaborated by telling them I had tried to ride two horses in my life and successfully fell off both of them.

The first horse was a Shetland Pony—the saddle had been cinched up on her but as I proceeded to mount, the saddle slipped under her belly, and so did I.

The second horse was an Arabian named "Silver"—I'll never forget it. It was my cousin's horse and she said, "You'll have no problem riding him." This time there wasn't a saddle. With her reassurance and assistance, I mounted Silver and proceeded cautiously. The longer I was on Silver, the more at home

I felt. We walked around, trotted a little, and then even galloped. I was so proud of myself. I was actually able to ride with no major problem. I decided to venture away from the farm a bit and we rode off into a nearby field. I stopped for a few minutes of rest, as my legs were beginning to tire. While I stopped, I could hear a horse off in another field neighing. Evidently Silver heard it also, for all of a sudden he lifted his head, opened his mouth, neighed back and took off. Naturally, Silver went one way and I went the other. My glasses flew off and I landed flat on my back.

I screamed with pain and I honestly thought I was dying. Luckily, my cousin was on her way to the field in a car to get me for lunch, and she saw what happened. She jumped out of the car and ran towards Silver. Silver stopped; she grabbed the reins and proceeded to scold him, and started to lead him towards my moaning body. All of a sudden, Silver stopped and wouldn't move another inch. She coaxed and scolded him, but he just wouldn't move at all. Finally, glancing near his front hooves, she noticed my glasses. After retrieving them, she was then able to lead him closer to me and to an area where she could tie him up. To make a long story short, I recovered nicely after a couple of weeks with nothing more than a very painful sprained back. To this day horses can sense the fear I have of them, no matter how hard I try.

After hearing my tale, my friends understood my fear but explained that many two year olds act that way in the paddock due to lack of schooling. They were somewhat doubtful that I was the cause of the horse's unruliness. Their words were comforting, but all I knew at that time was that it would be sometime before I stood close to the rail in the paddock again.

The sixth race of two year olds was already over by now, and I noticed the unruly one came in dead last. "Served him right," I thought, for scaring me like he did.

The seventh and eighth races were again profitable for me and at this time I started to think that maybe with some studying I might be able to make some additional money at this game.

Did I dare ask my friends one more question? Why not, I decided. "Do you know of any book I could purchase that would help me to understand more about this sport?" They thought for a moment and replied, "James N. Selvidge has a book out called 'Hold Your Horses'—that should help you." "Oh thanks, I'll pick one up as soon as I can. I promise I won't bother you anymore." They chuckled, and buried their heads in the Racing Form, again, for the ninth race was coming up. I just sat and watched as I figured I had enough excitement for the day, and since I still had money in my pocket, why not keep it for another day.

On Monday, at work, I spent my spare time explaining to the Doctor I worked for of my day's experience at the track. He was interested and stated that he enjoyed going, also. I then told him I was going to start studying the game and see if I could do any good at it. He wanted me to keep him informed of my progress.

That night after work I purchased a copy of "Hold Your Horses" and began studying my new challenge of racing. As I completed the book, my head was spinning with information. How was I going to remember everything? Was this challenge going to be more than I could handle? No way—I was determined to make a go of it.

Through the author's invitation, I joined the "Hold Your Horses Club," and from there I received literature regarding seminars and courses offered. I attended and read everything I could. Naturally, by this time I had met the author personally, and it was through his suggestion that I then joined the Horse Breeder's Women's Auxiliary in our area. I kept my eyes and ears opened to everything I could digest.

Six months had passed by. During that time I had kept the Doctor informed of my progress, and attended the track as much as I could. I was now keeping statistics on trainers' and jockeys' win percentages—post position wins, etc. Much to my disappointment, my bank account had not increased at all, and I felt like I had been neglecting my sons with all the time I was spending studying. Oh, I'd win here and there on spot plays, but nothing like I had anticipated. If I played the speed of the race, the pace horse would be the winner. If I played the front runner, a closer would win. Many races were won by horses that I couldn't figure at all. What was wrong? I just couldn't seem to put it all together. I was missing something, somewhere.

After a brief rest from the track, I set up an appointment with Mr. Selvidge, regarding his Handicapping Correspondence Course. I thought I needed to study some more before I continued my challenge, and I knew he could assist me. Our meeting was very enjoyable, and he invited me to join him at the races in the Turf Club the following day. Naturally, I accepted. Only a fool would have passed that up.

The next day at work, I just bubbled over with excitement just thinking about going to the races with a former breeder, owner and expert handicapper. The Doctor was happy to hear that I had graduated from the grandstand to the Turf Club. What a day—I could hardly wait for late afternoon and "Twilight Racing."

Dressed in my finery, I entered the Turf Club with Mr. Selvidge. I was now among the so called "High Rollers and Big Wigs." We sat at a table with a couple of Mr. Selvidge's associates. Everyone at the table had their head buried in a *Daily Racing Form.* Before the races, I had decided that I wasn't going to make any wagers at all, but just sit quietly and listen. Hopefully, I could learn how to put together everything I'd digested.

Before each race, one of Mr. Selvidge's associates would run downstairs to the paddock to check out the horses. He then would return and give some information to Mr. Selvidge. From this, Mr. Selvidge would make his decision and place his bets. His associate was telling Mr. Selvidge which horses were wearing tongue-ties. A tongue-tie—could this be the winning key? If this was in Mr. Selvidge's book, I certainly had forgotten all about it.

Before the next race his associate asked me if I'd care to walk out to the paddock and look at the horses with him. I very hesitantly accepted. In no way was I going to show them the fear that was about to engulf my body. Cautiously, I went, and was able to visually notice the tongue-ties that were being recorded. As we stood watching the horses, I noticed that my body wasn't trembling and my hands were dry. Could this be, was I finally able to control the fear I had? During the remaining races, I walked back and forth to the paddock making notes of different things I could see, and by the end of the day I felt very comfortable there. What a relief.

After the races Mr. Selvidge and I had dinner together; he requested that I start calling him "Jim," and asked if I'd care to join him again the following day. Of course I accepted, and continued to accept. If I had to work late I would join him at the track after work.

Early one morning during one of my "Thinking Sessions," it dawned on me that the racing power of a horse obviously comes from the back half of the horse. If a horse is worked-out properly, and enough, he should display some type of muscle, just as a weight lifter does. While at the races that same day, I began watching more closely the back half of the horse. I started first with the flank area. Sometimes it looked like jello, and other times I could see two or three bulges there. I tried to explain to Jim what I was seeing. I told him it looked just like "Tootsie Rolls" bulging out in the flank area. You should have heard him laugh. Here I was, a novice, explaining to a former owner, breeder, successful handicapper and author about "Tootsie Rolls." Was I crazy? I didn't think so. I kept track on my program with a capital "M" of every horse I saw go out with "Tootsie Rolls." I used the letter "M" for this I knew was muscle I was seeing on the horses. They didn't appear very often, but when I saw them I noticed the horses ran very well, and were always in the money.

One day I had decided to view the horses from the Turf Club windows instead of going down to the paddock each race. Believe me, that can really wear a person out. I'll never forget it. It was the sixth race—I saw a horse in the paddock with the biggest "Tootsie Rolls" I'd ever seen. The horse was beautiful, prancing, and with a beautiful shiny coat. It was absolutely breathtaking. Chills ran up and down my spine. "Oh my God, look at that horse." I was so embarrassed with the language I'd used. It just slipped out. Anyway, I ran quickly to Jim, and told him. "Oh, O.K." he said as his head remained in the *Daily Racing Form.* This time I could almost feel the horse was telling me to bet on him. I just couldn't resist. I went to the betting windows and put $10.00 across the board on my "Tootsie Roll" horse. I then noticed the father of the trainer of the horse that I'd just bet on. I walked over to him and said, "Your son's horse really looks good in this race." "Oh, do you think so? Do you think it can beat so and so?" as he was pointing to the *Daily Racing Form.* "We'll soon know, for there they go." I cannot describe in words the joy that I felt when my Tootsie Roll horse came across the finish line first, paying $52.10 to win. I was so excited and proud of myself. All my record keeping and observations were finally paying off. Jim, of course, was happy for me, but he had to admit that he didn't have a dime on the horse.

In the 8th and feature race that same day, another "Tootsie Roll" horse came out. Again, I went to Jim and told him. By this time, he was beginning to think that possibly there's something to the "Tootsie Roll" theory, and it would be worth at least a $2.00 wager. I, in turn, bet $10.00 across the board again. Yep, you betcha, my "Tootsie Roll" horse came flying across the finish line first, paying $18.20 to win. Not too shabby for a novice.

By this time, Jim had become a permanent fixture around my home, and that evening, as I presented my sons with a few $100.00 bills, they thought I was the greatest horse player and forgave me for all the time I'd spent on the horses instead of them. They commented, "Just keep it coming, Mom."

When I told the Doctor of my success at the track, he offered me a small bankroll to play for him the rest of the racing season. He said, "If I lost it all, it didn't matter, and if profitable, he'd split 50/50 with me." That sounded O.K. to me. I guess he was tired of hearing of my many stories of how I had seen the winners in the paddock and had all their positive signs recorded, but didn't bet on them because I was playing with "scared money." Especially Exacta's. I can't tell you how many winning Exacta's I sat through. I accepted the Doctors offer, and proceeded to build my confidence on picking winners with his money.

Each weekend, Jim would put on a Handicapping Breakfast for the public. He would give his selections for the day's card and discuss several angle plays. I naturally was introduced, and proceeded to give my analysis of how each horse looked the last time it raced, and would suggest different spot plays if the horse's appearance showed improvement. Jim, on several occasions, would discuss my "Tootsie Roll" theory. Many of the people who attended the breakfasts would stand next to me in the paddock and watch me take down my information. I was being plagued with questions. There's nothing more distracting then a bunch of questions while you're trying to concentrate, and listening to those famous horrible four words, "WHO DO YOU LIKE?"

On one of my good days, Jim had invited guests to join us in the Turf Club. I was doing my usual paddock inspection and we were doing O.K. One race I saw a horse that looked Super. He had a shiny, dappled coat, was prancing; his tail was arched; he was alert, responsive and had a stately looking appearance about him. It was just like he was saying, "Get out of my way fellows, this race is mine." On my return from the Paddock I stopped and made the largest wager I have ever made to this day, $50.00 to win. I couldn't believe what I had just done. $10.00 to win had been my highest wager up until then.

On the way to my seat I was stopped by an acquaintance of Jim's, who was an airplane pilot. He, in turn, asked me those delightful four words. I told him, and even showed him my win ticket to prove it. I also told him "if the horse wins, my fee is 10%." He laughed, and said, "What if he loses?" "He won't," I replied, feeling extremely confident. I returned to my seat—showed Jim and his guests my ticket and off they went to make their wagers. Jim was a little shocked to see the amount I wagered, and commented, "You must feel pretty sure of this one."

The race had started; the jockey had my horse in a good position—"just don't tire him out," I thought. Into the stretch drive they came—my horse was racing head and head with another. I stood up—my heart was pounding—my hands were wet, and my body was shaking something awful. It was a photo finish—"Did he win?—Did he win?" I asked. I couldn't really tell. Jim tried to calm me down, and reassured me that he had. It had to be the longest photo finish that I had ever stood through. I was shaking so badly, I stood holding on to a metal railing trying to keep myself up. The Lord only knows why I didn't sit down. I guess I wanted to be the first one to see the final results.

I waited and waited—all I could think about was all those people I had touted on my horse. He just had to have won. Finally, the race was official, and I won, with a payoff of $17.20 to win. I slowly collapsed into my seat, my body was still shaking and the tears just rolled down my face. Jim put his comforting arms around me and said, "You won, honey! You won!" Jim's guests remarked, "Gosh, this is just like the movies," as they shook my hand. Believe me, it took a good hour for me to calm down. On my way to the cashiers window, the airplane pilot caught up to me, thanked me for the tip, and remarked that he'd made over $1,800.00 on the race and wanted to buy me a drink as payment. I was furious. "A drink! You know what you can do with that drink don't you! What about my 10%?" He proceeded to tell me his sob story about how his wife left him and took everything. "That certainly wasn't my fault was it?" I guess I was pretty rude, but darnit, I'd been studying for a long time and I felt it was about time I got paid for what I knew. He then offered me a $50 dollar bill, and since that is what I bet, I decided that that was O.K. I did decide at that time, if he ever asked me those famous words again, he'd never get any information out of me.

By the end of that racing season I was able to return a healthy bankroll to the Doctor. He was delighted and took his lovely wife on a small trip with his share of the profits.

In 1983, Jim was asked to be a speaker at the Handicapping Expo '83 Conference in Los Angeles. Naturally, I made arrangements with the Doctor to take my vacation at the same time. Since we were going to be in California, Jim decided to kill two birds with one stone and scheduled seminars for the two of us at Bay Meadows and Del Mar after the Conference. He would speak on Handicapping techniques and Money Management, and I would give instructions on Paddock Inspection at the track.

While at the Handicapping Conference, Jim's schedule was so tight, and was in such need of my assistance, that I was not able to attend any sessions other than his.

The Conference was over, and our next stop was Del Mar. There our Seminar went very well. At the track I was able to point out and explain a great deal to those who participated. The horses were all in excellent form. I did notice that about 75% of the winners were dappled—so these were the horses we played.

Our next stop was Bay Meadows for the beginning of the Fair Meet racing season. Again, our Seminar went well. While at the track, through one of our Paddock Inspection sessions, I was explaining to the students that often, if one watches the tractor go by on the track during maintenance, they can actually tell which lanes are being plowed deeper than the others. As I pointed out on one race, we could plainly see that lanes 1, 2, & 3 were being plowed pretty deep. I advised my students to look for stamina breeding in the race. Glancing through the program, I noticed that there was only one horse that fit that description, and it was sired by McARTHUR PARK. He was scheduled to race in post position #5. I then told everyone to watch this horse carefully as he entered the paddock. If his body signs were positive, he should be a bet. While viewing the horse for that race the 1, 4, 5, & 12 horses were all displaying positives. I suggested that they bet the 5 horse, and if they played Exacta's, they should box all four of them. We then went our separate ways to wager, and I located Jim eating lunch with a friend. Time was running short, and I kept telling Jim to box the 1, 4, 5, & 12. I repeated it about three times. Finally, when he realized I was serious, and proceeded to excuse himself, it was too late. The #5 horse won, paying $83.40 to win. The #1 horse was second, and the Exacta paid $739.00.

When returning to the paddock for the next race, I found only one student had the guts to bet on my 40 to 1 shot. He had bet $2.00 across the board, and made enough to pay for the cost of the Seminar. He was extremely grateful. Naturally, the rest of us, including Jim, were not experiencing that same feeling at all. That $83.40 was the highest price horse I'd ever recommended.

I seldom checked the odds of a horse. If the horse looked the part in the paddock, I usually bet it.

Jim and I parted in California. I had to return to my job, and he had decided to relocate his business to Las Vegas. We had planned that I would move to Vegas with him as soon as I could get a replacement for the Doctor, and also after my youngest son had graduated.

During the following year, I continued my paddock inspection at the track and held seminars on my own in Washington and Oregon.

In September of 1984 I had everything situated to where I could move to Las Vegas and be with Jim. Playing the races at a Race Book is a whole different story and we'll go into that later.

In November of 1984, Jim was again asked to be a speaker at the Handicapping Expo Conference in New Jersey. Jim had pre-arranged for us to do two different seminars while we were back there, one in New Jersey and one in New York, again killing two birds with one stone.

At the Conference, I was able to attend a session conducted by Ms. Bonnie Ledbetter. She was speaking on the body language of horses. Her session was informative, but based more for the owner, breeder and trainer. I was looking for information for the Handicapper.

During each evening after the conference, we were all bussed to Meadowlands Race Track, and Ms. Ledbetter would give her analysis of each horse as they passed by. I sat a couple of seats away from her, and with pen in hand I began to record everything she said. I began to note some discrepancies. As the horses entered the paddock, she would state a particular horse was "Fit and Ready." After it was saddled the horse was specified a throw-out. "What is this, I thought? She's getting the horses mixed up. She's not writing anything down—how can she remember correctly?" People were constantly asking her what she thought of different horses, and I could see she needed help. So the next time she was asked, I volunteered the information. She looked at my program and couldn't believe everything I'd recorded. She then asked me if I'd please sit by her, and assist her for the rest of the races. I agreed.

One evening I explained a little to Bonnie about the work Jim and I were doing regarding superior speed horses and how we were tracking them all over the United States. We had already played several at Meadowlands and they were winning, paying nice prices. She became more and more interested. She wanted to know if there was anyway she could get the speed horses for Turf Paradise. I said, "Yes, but you'll have to call me each week in Las Vegas with the race results as they have to be figured on our computer. After that I will call you back with the information." She agreed, and from then on our friendship grew.

In 1985, I was requested to lecture at a paddock inspection Seminar near Arlington Park in Chicago, sponsored by Midwest Track Analysts, Inc. I suggested to the organizer that possibly I could get Bonnie to speak, also. I called her; we discussed her fees, and we agreed to do our first seminar together. Bonnie is an excellent speaker. We worked together well, and our seminar was successful. We were given the red carpet treatment. We were escorted to Sportsman's Park to watch the harness races, as well as Balmoral Park for more Thoroughbred racing. Three weeks after we returned, we watched Arlington Park burn to the ground on T.V. We just couldn't believe it.

In March of 1986, we were invited to lecture in Florida near Hialeah Park. The seminar was sponsored by Florida Turf Analysts, Inc. Bonnie and I had a terrible time making our plane connections and when we finally arrived, we were exhausted. However, the red carpet was again out for us.

The first evening consisted of a three hour lecture in which we both took part. Early the following morning, we went to the track (Hialeah Park) to watch the morning workouts. Here Bonnie pointed out horses changing leads, and proper strides. That afternoon all seminar participants met us at the track for a day at the races. They were separated into two groups, half of them were with me learning paddock inspection and the other half with Bonnie in box seats listening to her comments regarding the post parade. When the races were half over, the two groups switched places. Our seminars go well this way, as long as my feet hold out.

On our last day at Hialeah, we were giving some advanced tutoring to the president and vice president of F.T.A. My feet were giving out, so I suggested we join Bonnie for a couple of races and watch the Post Parade. It was the fifth race; the horses had paraded in front of us, and had turned around and were on their way back. All of a sudden, I noticed a horse with "Tootsie Rolls." I said, "number seven is tight in the flanks." I glanced at my program and noticed the sire of my #7 was the same as the sire of the horse that had just won the previous race. HORSES FOR COURSES, I thought.

I rushed to the windows and placed a wager on #7. I guess I don't need to tell you who got the hand shakes after #7 came across the finish line first, paying $35.20.

In 1987 my teaching continued locally, lecturing at the Senior Turf Club luncheons, and at the Palace Station Casino as guest speaker for Pat Rogerson's, "Between The Races" program.

In 1988 my better half was able to raise a group of wonderful investors to assist in the expense of the filming of my first video.

Through my authorship a woman contacted me and made several wonderful comments on my book. Since then we have corresponded, visited, and played the horses together several times. She is totally responsible for introducing me to my video producer, who is the finest most inventive equine specialist available.

Another friend invited me to a Saturday morning workout program at Golden Gate. She, too, is a new found friend from my authorship. Being in the area, I decided to go. After the workout program (which I feel is important for all to attend whenever possible) we had the opportunity to visit the backside. Here we were taken to a stable by a delightful young exercise rider and introduced to much of what the horse encounters on the backside. I was so impressed with his honesty and straight forwardness that I had my friend introduce me to him after the program was finished. I gave him my card and told him of my intent to do a video on my book, and that my desire would be to introduce much of what he had just discussed. I asked him if he would be interested in participating and he said sure. I thought, "wow, does he really mean it?" When I arrived back in Vegas, I immediately mailed a copy of my book to him to review. Well, much to my delight, he called and said he thought my book was great and he'd be happy to work on a video with me. I couldn't believe it. He suggested that we contact Bay Meadows Race Track for the filming, for he had now gotten his trainers license and was training there.

By letter and much waiting we finally got approval from Bay Meadows to allow us to film on dark days (days that there is no racing going on) only. This I could work with, for I didn't want a lot of people around while filming anyway.

So, on July 11, 1988 we started our first day of filming. Flying in the day before, and not sleeping due to a strange bed, is not a way to become a star. Being overly tired on your very first shooting in front of a camera is not the way to impress your producer or film crew. Then, the good Lord blessed us with a healthy wind that we had to contend with as well as many airplanes flying overhead. Let me tell you though, it was an experience.

I'm not going to tell you "my trainer's" name but I do want to tell you a little bit about him. He is one who "cares" about fans, and what is good for racing. He is one of those 30% winners with a purposefully small stable, and consequently is invisible in terms of the *Daily Racing Form* trainer standings. The reason I'm not telling you his name is because I sincerely feel you should watch the video and then you'll find out who he is. Even if you don't own a VCR it would be well worth it to rent one just to see it. Much of what you'll read in this book is so much easier to understand when you see it on the screen. Besides, seeing is believing.

Now, we are trying to pull together material for the second video. This one, too, will be extremely valuable to you. Once this is completed, my better half and I will be traveling to several different tracks introducing the videos and doing seminars. Hopefully, we'll be seeing you at your local track soon. If you would be interested in arranging such an affair, please contact me.

I pledge to those of you that are just beginning to play horses, and to you old timers, to reveal all information that I have collected through my studies. I only hope I don't forget anything. I am trying to write this as simply as possible in hopes that you'll be able to see and hear the horses talk to you. I sincerely hope the information to follow will assist all readers in many trips to the cashier's window.

II.
CONFORMATION

CONFORMATION

A horse player would do well to think of the Thoroughbred as a professional athlete. A slight grasp of equine anatomy, problems and signposts can allow the player to weed out the good from the bad.

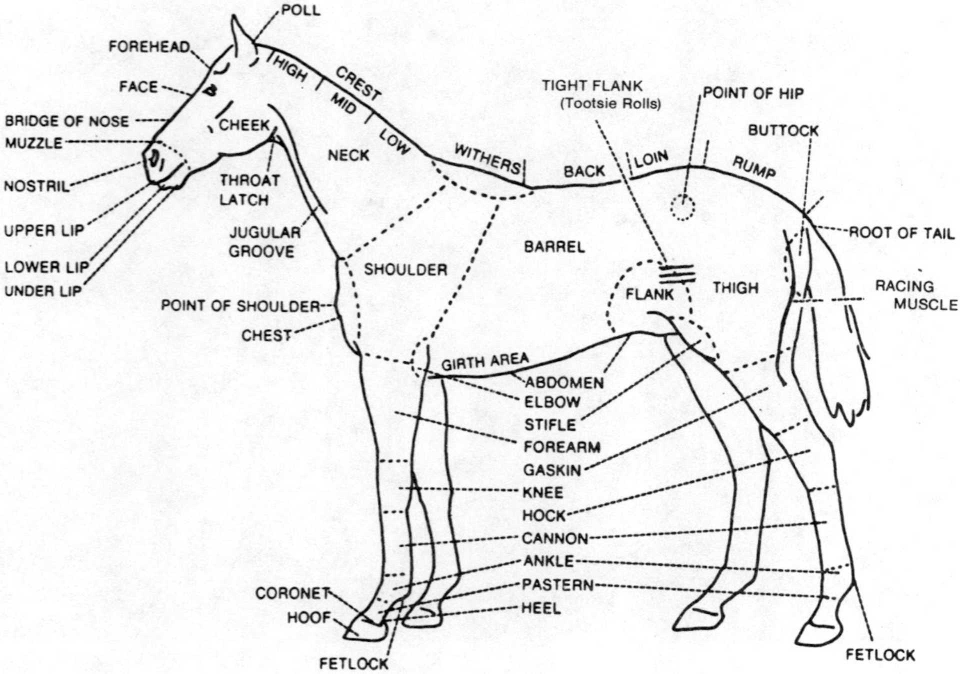

The ideal race horse should have a lean, small head, with big, well set eyes, small muzzle and big jaw, ears tapered; the neck long and set into a gradual sloped shoulder; thin high withers and a deep, full breast. The back should have just enough room for a saddle, connecting with great hind quarters. The front legs should be straight with short cannons, and the hind legs, extremely broad down to the hocks.

CONFORMATION PERFECTION

Steve Stidham

When I first viewed the above picture I thought to myself, that sure looks like a horse I should know. I literally got those chills again just looking at it. The conformation of this magnificent equine specimen is perfect. Look at those front legs how straight they are. Can you imagine the power this horse could exert with hind quarters that size? Look how broad the hind legs are to the hocks. Now I know you would like to know who this horse is. Of course, it's JOHN HENRY!

THE GOOD, BAD, AND THE UGLY

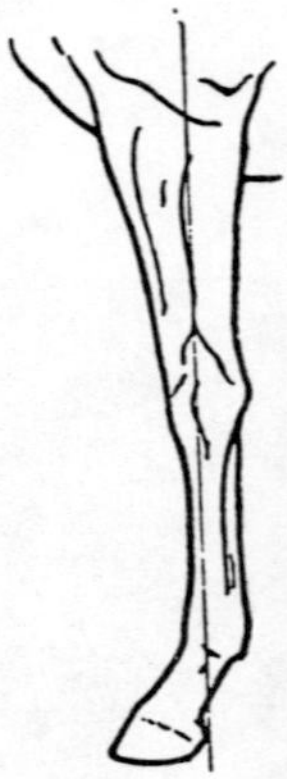

The Forelegs—Side View

GOOD FORELEG

A good foreleg will be straight, with tendons that run behind the cannon well set out from the bone. The pasterns should slope at a 45 degree angle, and not be too long or too short. They should look as if weight is being distributed equally between the bony column of the pasterns and the tendons.

CALF-KNEED

Back at the knees, also called calf-kneed, will look as if the leg is angled backwards. This conformation fault will cause severe strain on the knee and the horse will probably have a very short racing career.

OVER AT THE KNEE

The forelegs of a horse whose knees look as if they are buckling forward is called "over at the knee" or "buck-kneed." Because of the nature of the downward pressure in each stride, this kind of knee is usually less vulnerable to injury. But the horse with this conformation must first show that he can stride effectively.

CALF-KNEED

Unknown

Can you see the conformation fault in this horse? The foreleg that is on the track is calf-kneed. See how it curves backwards? The weight of this horse looks like it could snap the knee at any time. Even though he won this particular race, his racing career was very short. I have yet to figure out where the left front hoof of this horse is.

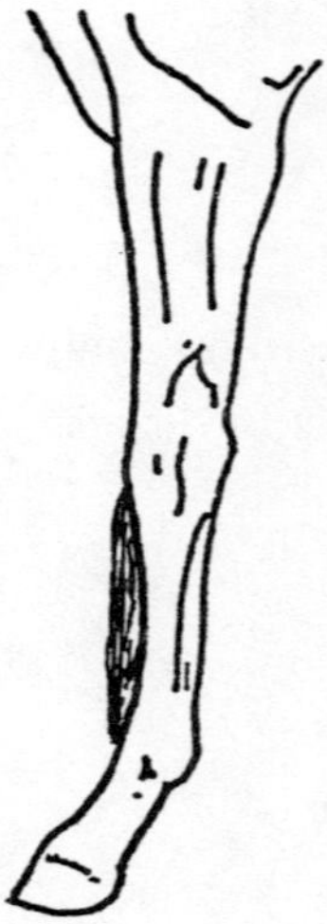

BUCKED SHINS

The inflammation of the membrane surrounding the cannon bone is called periostitis. It is more commonly known in racing as "bucked shins." It is common in young Thoroughbreds during the first few weeks of training, but shouldn't have to happen if trained properly. It comes from the concussion of running on hard tracks as well as immature legs. Rest is essential if complete recovery is to occur.

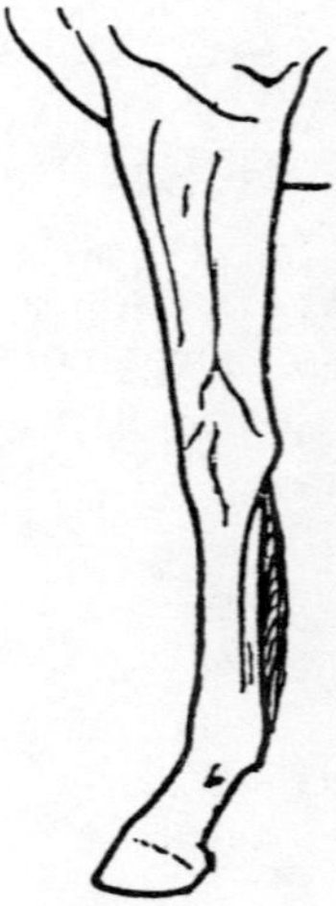

BOWED TENDON

The inflammation caused by the tearing loose of the flexor tendons running along the cannon bone is called a "bowed tendon." Fluids fill in the damaged area causing the swelling and the bowed appearance. This severe strain injury should be treated with support bandages, anti-inflammatories and rest for up to at least a year. The good winner ROO ART suffered a bowed tendon and was retired soon after.

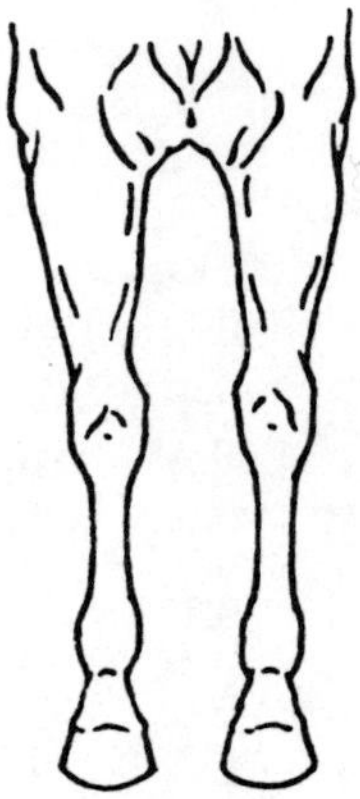

The Forelegs—Front View

GOOD

A Thoroughbred with straight front forelegs will be able to stride effectively, reaching out in an even gate.

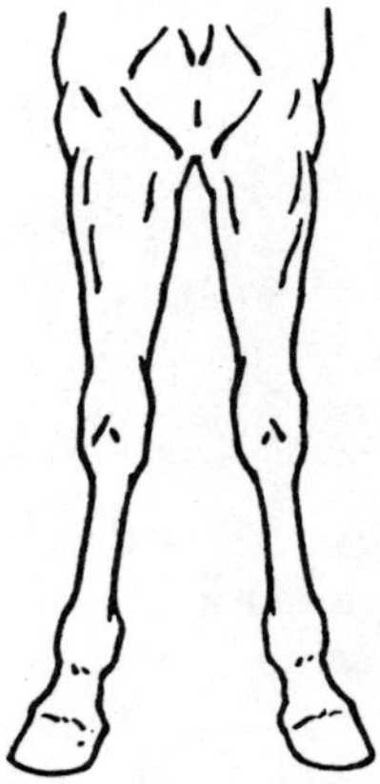

SPLAYED FEET & KNOCK KNEES

Horses whose forelegs are shaped causing the hooves to turn outward will have a tendency to "wing" or "airplane," and will not stride effectively. A Horse with this fault can cut or trip a horse running too close at his side.

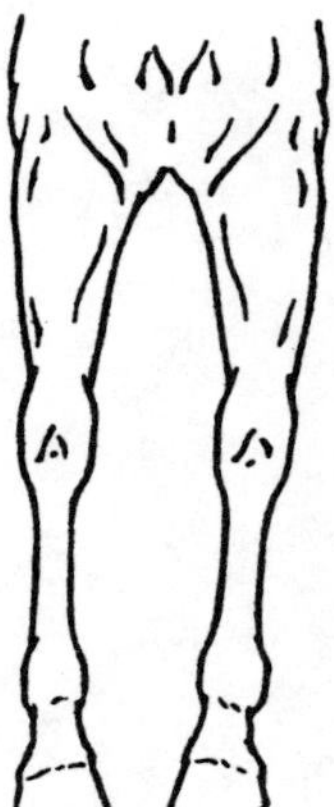

TOEING-IN

Horses whose forelegs are formed causing the hooves to turn inward will have a tendency to "paddle." A horse with this trait may injure himself. Whether splayed or toeing-in the legs will be moving in an inefficient circular arc when striding.

TOEING-IN	TOEING-OUT
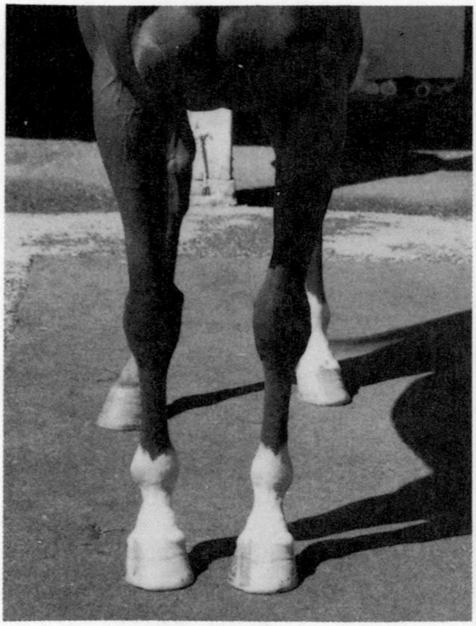	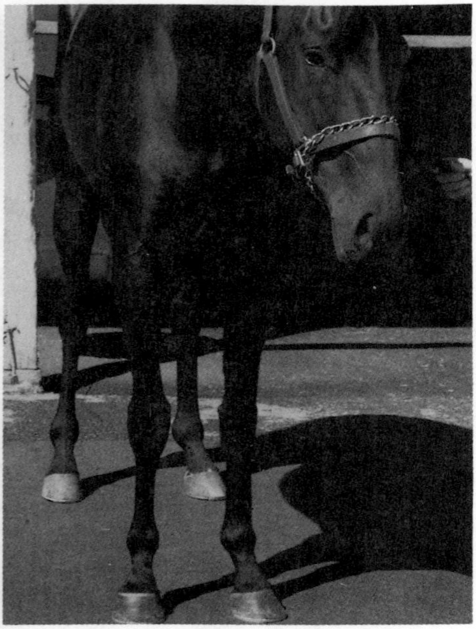
Millard Richards	*Millard Richards*

Both toeing-in and toeing-out are not suited for a straight forward movement, or for the most advantageous use of the fore feet in maintaining the balance of the body in motion. If I'm at a small track, I may see races where all of the horses may have this conformation fault. In this case, I will bet a horse that has other very positive body signs. Even at Santa Anita, this is possible in the cheapest claiming races. But anytime purses are high, and well-conformed horses are entered I would eliminate horses that "toe-in" or "toe-out." When you look at their running action, you know they will not be able to run as fast as a good horse, or sustain speed for the whole race against the better athlete.

The Hind Legs—Side View

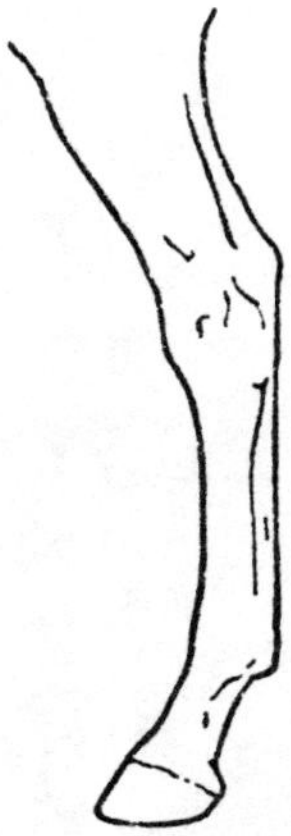

GOOD

Imagine a plumb line hanging from the base of the tail. The hind legs should be straight and vertical to this imaginary line.

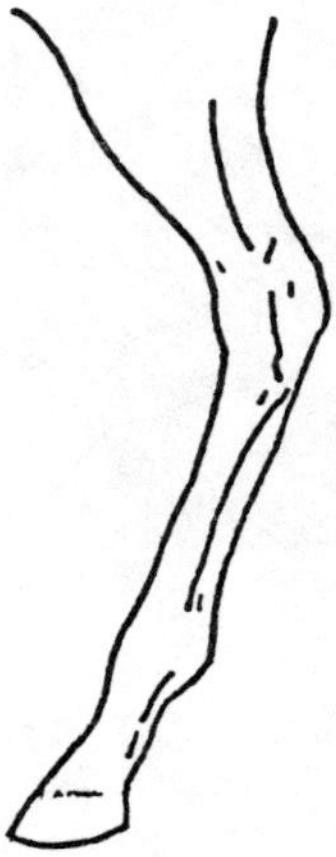

SICKLE HOCK

At rest, a horse who looks like he is standing under himself has "sickle hocks." A horse with this condition will never be quick at the starting gate and it can cause strain in young horses. This trait is often desired in Europe because so much of their racing is on the grass.

CAPPED HOCKS

The hind legs with capped or curb hocks indicates a painful swelling and thickening of one or all of the ligaments or tendons at the lower part of the hock. This condition is more often found in horses with sickle hocks, and usually comes from kicking in horse vans or in stalls.

The Hind Legs—Rear View

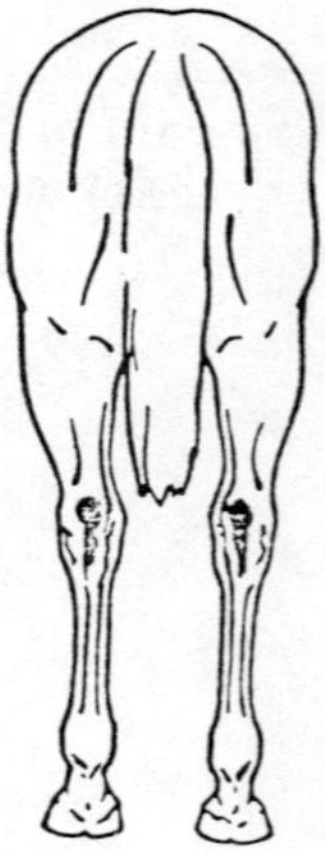

GOOD

Horses whose rear legs are in a straight line from the point of the hocks to the fetlock and with hooves pointing straight forward will race with great strength.

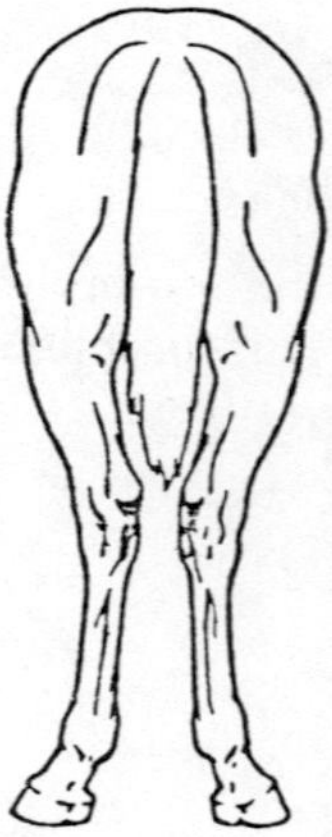

COW HOCKED

A horse who is cow hocked will show the points of the hocks being turned in, with rear hooves turning out. This is a conformation fault where the hocks are very close to each other.

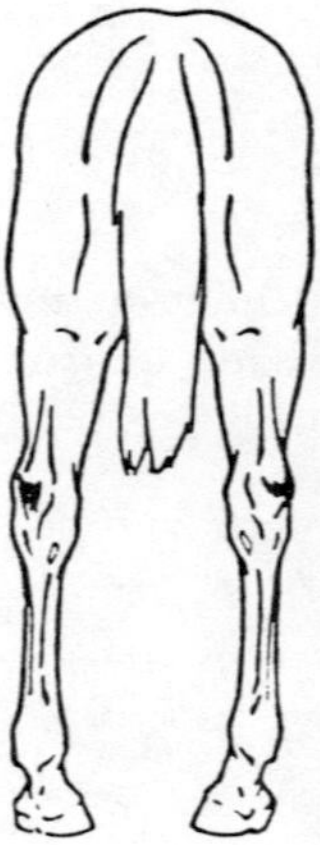

HOCKS TURNED OUT

Hocks turned out, naturally will show the points of the hocks turning out, with rear hooves pointed inward. The rear hooves will appear to be pigeon-toed.

THE CHEST

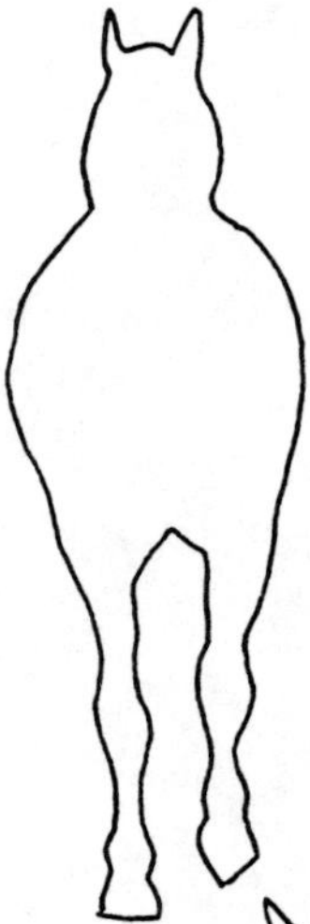

This horse is built correctly with respect to conformation. Each leg will be brought forward in a straight line and will have a better chance of not injuring himself with his own action.

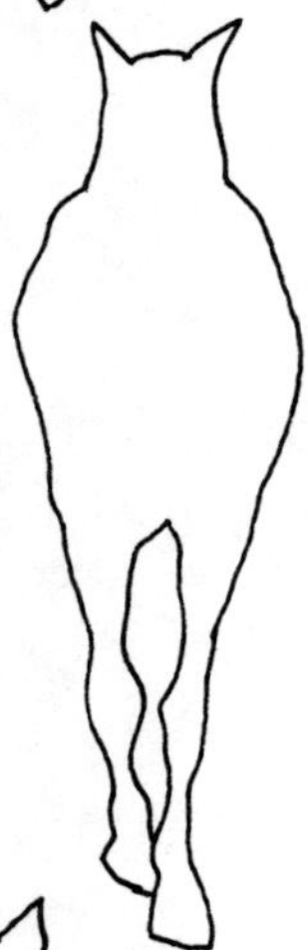

A very narrow chest can cause the horse to interfere with himself when running. This problem will especially occur when he becomes tired.

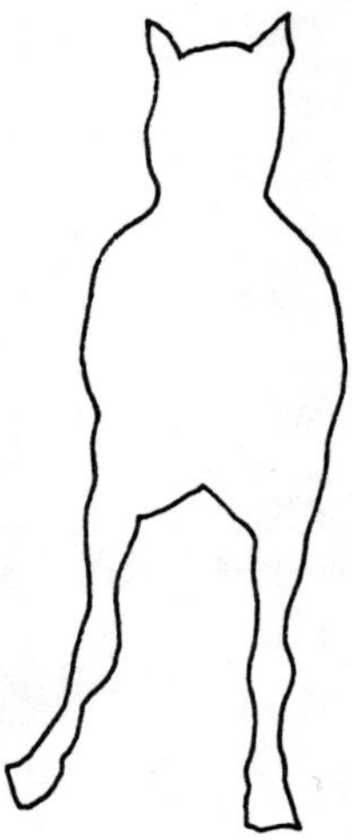

A horse with a very wide chest will have a tendency to paddle when moving, an action characterized by the outward rotation of the leg from the elbow.

THE HOOF

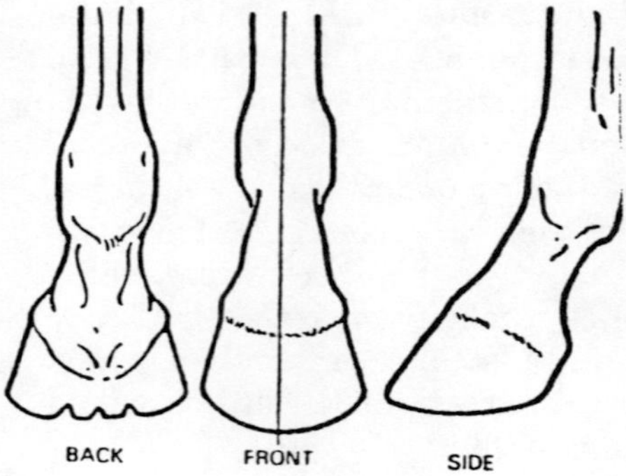

The hoof of the horse is comparable to the nail of our middle finger or toe. The horse actually stands on tip-toe, on his middle toenail. It should be bell shaped and smooth on the outside. The thicker and tougher the toe wall is, the better. If there's no wall, there is no way the farrier can attach a shoe. The hoof grows like a fingernail and is usually trimmed and shod about every three to five weeks. A conditioner or mud pack should be applied frequently to the foot, to prevent drying and hardening.

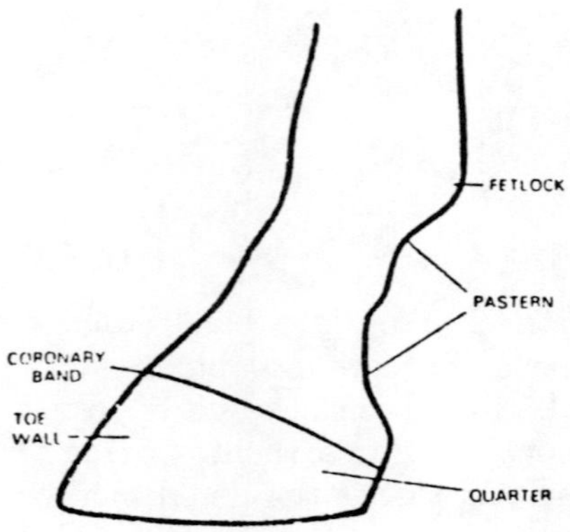

CORONARY BAND—This is a soft band, something like our cuticle, encircling the foot just above the hoof.

FETLOCK—This is a joint on both the front and hind legs that corresponds to our knuckles.

PASTERN—The pastern is two bones, an upper and lower, with a joint between. These, with their ligaments, act as a shock absorber when the foot hits the ground.

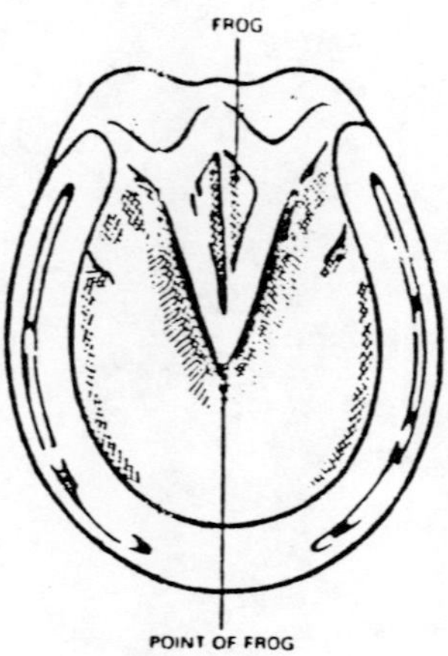

FROG—The inside of the hoof is concave with a V-shaped mass of flesh in the middle of the sole called a frog. The frog acts as a cushion with each step the horse takes, even when he is wearing shoes. It also supplies the blood circulation to the hoof with every stride. An injury to the frog is literally crippling.

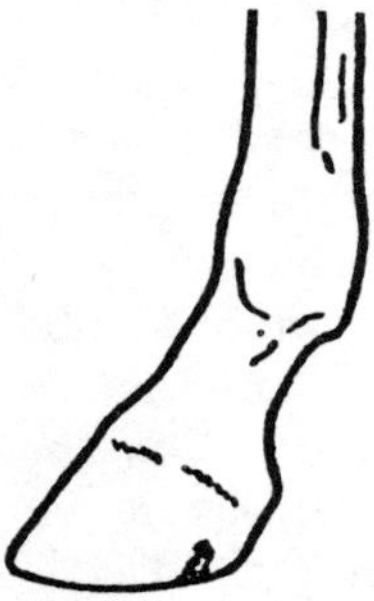

QUARTER CRACK—A crack on the side of the horny wall of the hoof is called a quarter crack. It can cause short term lameness. It is caused from the loss of too much moisture in the hoof, thus becoming dried out and contracted. It often occurs in dry weather or as a result of poor grooming. A horse can cause injury to his hoof while being playful or rambunctious. One hoof may accidentally stomp on another which causes a quarter crack. This is called "grabbing a quarter."

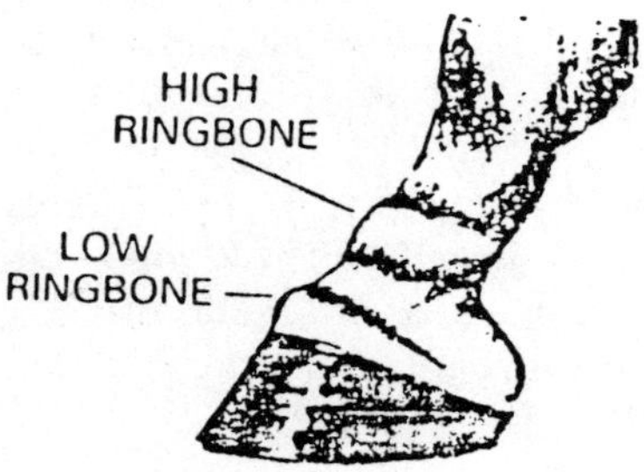

RING BONE—This is a bony enlargement above the coronary band and/or slightly higher. It is the result of periostitis and may lead to arthritis. Firing or blistering and rest is the usual method of treatment.

BOOTS

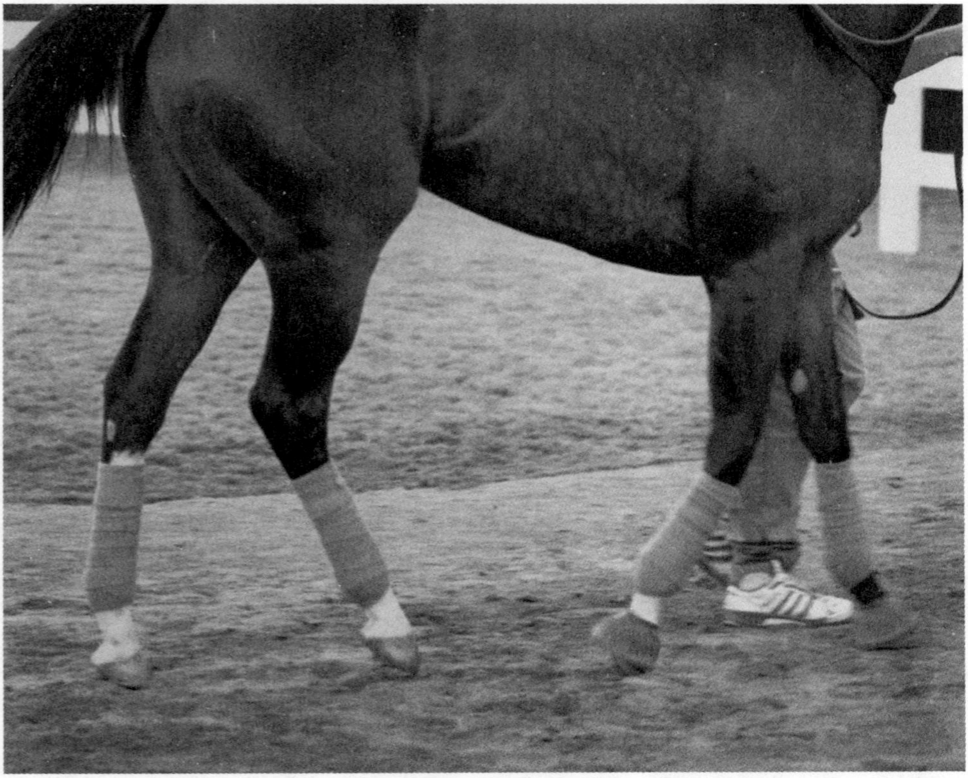

Steve Stidham

Notice the front hooves of this horse. He is wearing boots. These are called bell boots and are worn for protection only. You will not see a horse race in boots such as these. Often a horse will get playful and jump around a lot. These boots will protect a horse from grabbing a quarter, or will protect one that already has a quarter crack.

III.
SIGNPOSTS TO FITNESS AND FORM

SIGNPOSTS TO FITNESS AND FORM

"Fitness" and "Form" are major contributors to the winner's circle. Once you are able to detect the physical signposts of muscle tone, strength, health and spirit, it will seem like the horses are talking to you. The head, eyes, ears, mouth, legs, feet, tail and body all have distinct characteristics that can be interpreted. Once you've absorbed the drawings and descriptions in this chapter, you'll find yourself one step closer to the cashiers' windows.

Learning the positive and negative physical signposts of the horse is not an easy task. Do not expect to pick it up in a day or so. Generally, I find that women are able to pick it up much faster than men. Don't get me wrong, though, some of my better students are men, and do extremely well.

THE HEAD

The head of a winner will be held in a stately manner moving calmly in different directions to satisfy his curiosity. A lean, small head contributes to the looks and balance of a horse.

The up and down movement of the head is a positive, especially if the horse is reaching forward with his mouth. Be careful here, some up and down movement may be caused from the jockey holding the reins too tight, thus causing discomfort from the bit. Be sure, when you see this movement, that the reins are loose.

During the post parade, if you see a horse shove his head (nose) into the neck of the lead pony, (as if he were trying to push the lead pony to go faster) this is a definite positive, and should be wagered on.

The hanging, or side to side bobbing head, is a negative signpost and signifies soreness. The head will bob to the opposite side of the pain endured.

The high held tossing head, signifies anger and fear. This negative signpost can be re-confirmed in the post parade as the horse will probably have his head over the neck of the lead pony. Often, you'll see a halter with a chain shank used for control. The chain will be seen either over the nose or up under the upper lip. Sometimes even a twitch is used on the young, fearful, and inexperienced horses. This also is a negative, especially if the mouth is cut and bleeding.

The head displaying bulging veins is a sign of exhaustion.

FEARFUL

Curt Carlson

This horse's high-held head indicates he is fearful of something. The whites of his eyes are almost visible. The head collar used has a chain shank over the nose. This assists the handler in controlling any unruly movement. The head collar is naturally removed before racing. Horses that are truly terrified of racing stay that way race after race—until and unless the trainer can work some miracle to straighten out the mental basket case. A truly frightened horse can be dangerous when being saddled, and again when the jockey is mounting.

SPOOKED

Steve Stidham

This horse appears to be "spooked." The degree of fright or terror can be measured by how much we see of the white of the eye. What we see in this picture tells us many things. This horse has no halter with a chain shank on it, so he probably doesn't have an overall "head problem." Note the ears—they are forward. He may be frightened or surprised by (a strange looking object suddenly raised up by a stranger—the cameraman), but he is also interested. I would watch this horse in the post parade and with binoculars on the backstretch. If an incident really scared him, I would expect to see sweat, and other negative signs, as he progressed to the starters gate. More likely, this horse will be quite calm by then. Look at the mane of this horse. Is he so scared his mane curled? I think not. Bulging veins on neck could indicate exhaustion.

ALERT AND INTERESTED

Steve Stidham

This horse is extremely interested and alert. The ears are perked forward and he obviously is very well mannered. The head collar that is used here has a chain shank but the chain is covered with a rubber substance that will not injure the horse in anyway. Check it out, the horse is smiling at you.

THE EYES

The Thoroughbred has monocular vision. This vision is like a wide-angled camera, which allows the horse to see all the way behind him. Unlike humans, his eyes are placed on the sides of his head. Each eye observes differently; the left eye views surroundings on the left side and the right eye views on the right side. The position of the horse's head changes the focus of his eyes. He has to concentrate to focus on objects in front of him. Frontal focus is preferred in racing and blinkers do help keep the eyes focused ahead.

The positive eyes to look for are big, prominent, lustrous eyes. They are a sign of good health. If they are wide-set, he is a safer mount because he can see farther behind and is less likely to shy at imaginary dangers.

The eyes of a horse who is suffering with internal pain or drugged with a depressant (downer), will be glazed and unresponsive.

A horse drugged with a stimulant (upper) will have glassy bulging eyes.

A frightened horse's eyes will roll and the whites will become visible. They will not be focused on anything; a definite negative.

THE EARS

The horse's ears have a variety of expressions, to convey a mood or draw attention to an object, and often give warning signals. They are easily viewed whether watching them at the paddock, in the walking ring or during the post parade either at the track or at a race book thru simulcasting. There are five responses to watch for.

1–THE ALERT RESPONSE–(positive)

The ears of the horse rotate somewhat more than 180 degrees and thus pull in sounds from every direction. The openings will rotate in the direction that the sound is coming from. Forward-pricked ears means a forward-going happy horse.

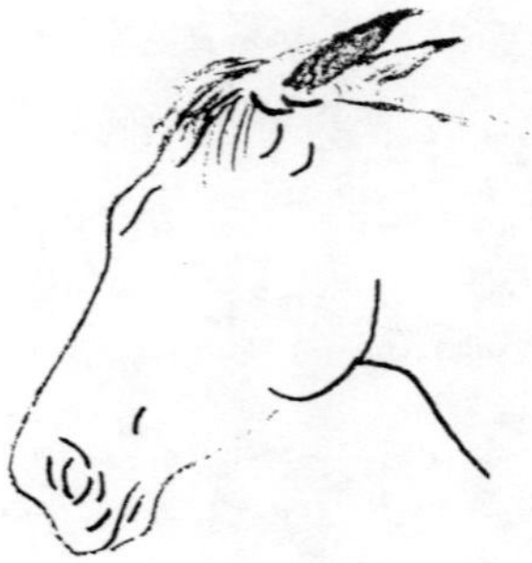

2–THE ANGRY RESPONSE–(negative) MAD

A flattened ear, back against the neck, usually indicates violent action–a kick, or a bite. The longer the ears are back the more unhappy or angry he/she is. Any discomfort, such as a jerk on the bit or the first feel of the whip will cause the ears to pin back.

3–THE FRIGHTENED RESPONSE–(negative)

The ears are not focused on any particular thing. They will constantly be twitching in every direction. A horse with this response will almost never be in the winner's circle.

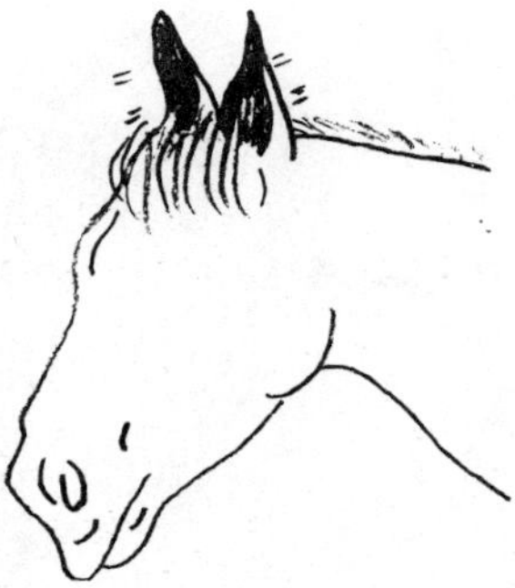

4—THE FROZEN RESPONSE—(positive or negative)

The ears do not move in any direction at all. This horse has been given a stimulus drug (upper) that causes this reaction. Often this horse will have a tendency to washout by the time it gets to the gate. Betting or passing the race hinges to the racing stable. Drugged horses do win, but many do not. There is risk of the horse breaking down.

5—THE AIRPLANE RESPONSE

The ears are down and flopped sideways. This can be a sign of drugs (downer), a horse medicated with a depressant. This horse will look very lazy and almost asleep.

FRONT VIEW

SIDE VIEW

ALERT RESPONSE

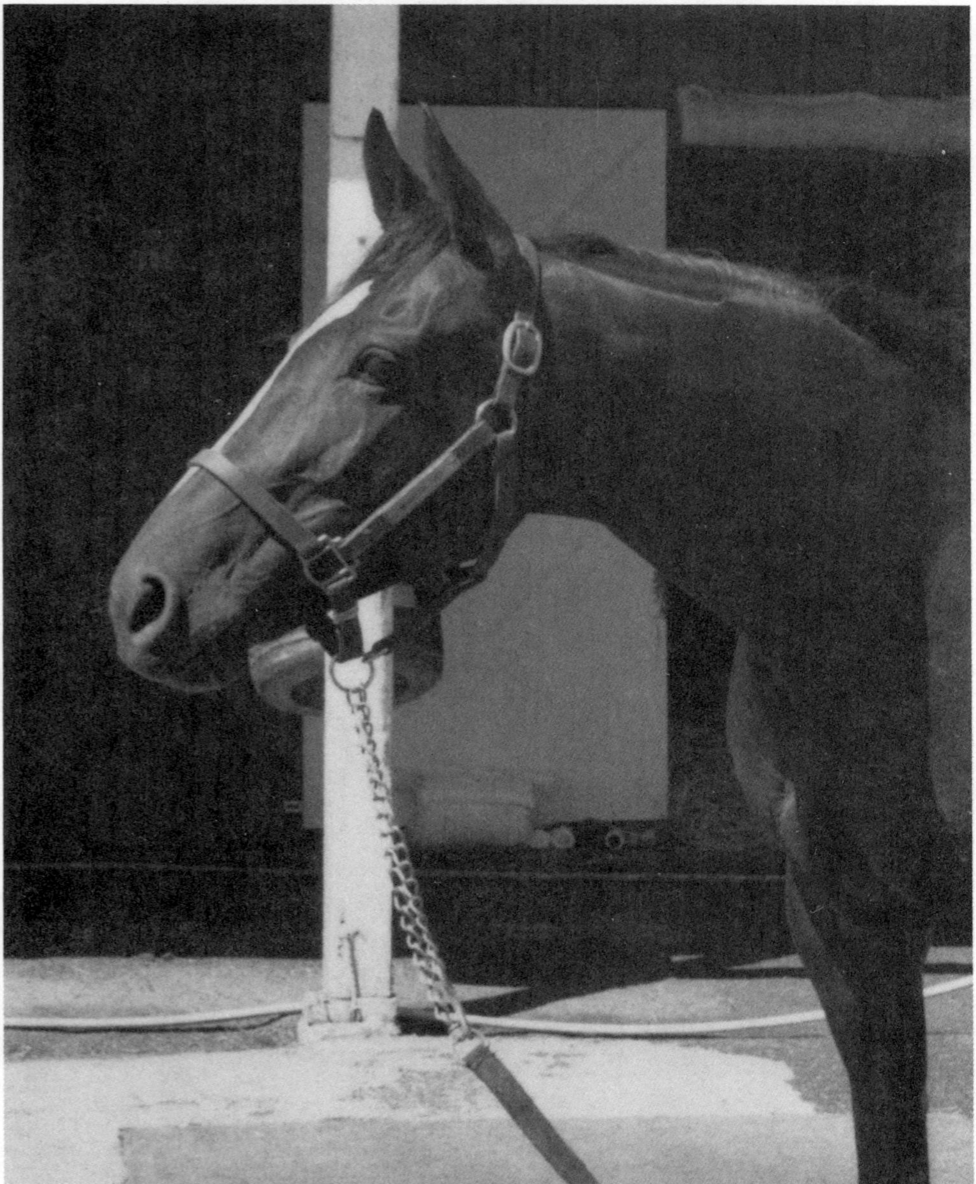

Millard Richards

The ears of this horse are perked forward. This is an alert response. Very positive when it comes to wagering. Note how well-mannered this one is. The halter is used, but no one has to use the chain shank on him. I'll bet there's a blue bird a short distance away singing him a song.

ANGRY RESPONSE

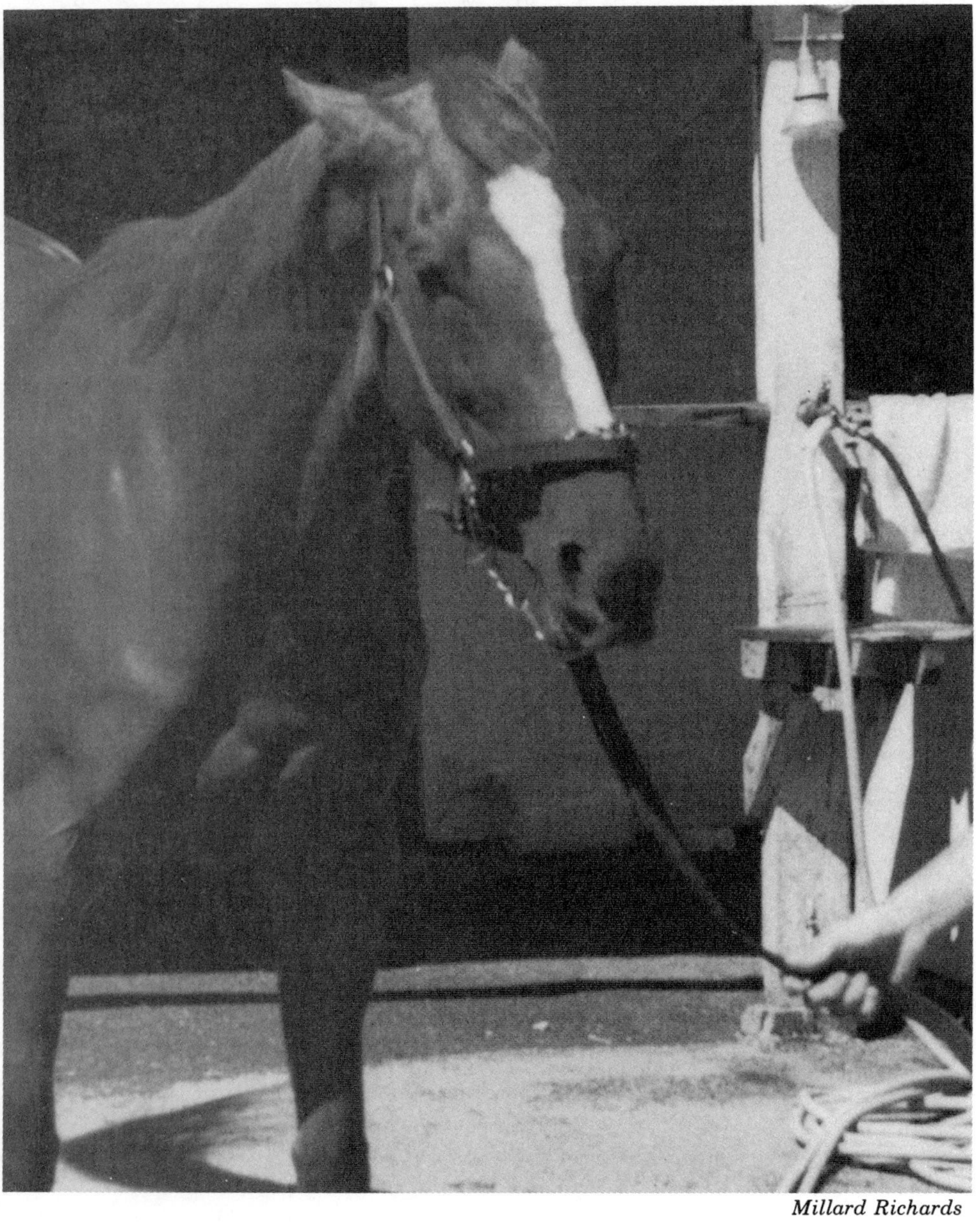

Millard Richards

This poor baby is mad about something. Maybe someone is annoying him. Could it be? Those ears are sure flattened back to his head. The longer they are back the madder he is. The handler here chooses to use the chain shank over the nose on this one. I personally would too.

THE TONGUE

The tongue of the horse, whether long or short, may be the cause of a positive or negative racing style. Many horses "play" with their tongues even with a bit on. If a horse gets his tongue over his bit he is difficult to guide. Other horses, while racing, have a tendency to "swallow" their tongues and therefore cut off the throat's air passage and partially choke.

A horse breathes through his nose not his mouth.

THE TONGUE TIE—(positive)

Tying the horse's tongue to the bottom of his/her jaw assists the horse a great deal. The jockey has less difficulty holding the horse in, and by no longer being able to play with his tongue, the horse is more apt to keep his mind on racing.

The tongue is usually tied with a strip of cloth (usually white) which you'll be able to see hang from his chin. Some trainers are very tricky, and will tie them with a leather strap, using the same color as the horse. This is extremely difficult to spot unless you're standing right at the paddock.

The tongue tie also signifies trainer intent. If you keep records of trainers and horses who use tongue ties, you will definitely increase your win percentage. For instance, if you know a horse has won a race previously with a tongue tie—and now you see the same horse without one—I would definitely not bet the horse.

It has been rumored, that some trainers soak their tongue ties in a solution of some sort. When allowed to dry, and inserted into the horse's mouth, their saliva dissolves the substance just in time to provide a winning burst of speed.

TONGUE-TIE

Steve Stidham

This horse is wearing a white gauze tongue-tie. Can you see it passing through the mouth and under the chin? The tongue is held and a white gauze-like strap is wrapped around the tongue once, and then tied under the chin. **Note: The tongue is hanging outside the mouth of this horse, and this would be a negative.** *The tongue-tie with the tongue inside the horses mouth is a positive.*

THE COAT

The coat of the horse is the most highly visible part of the anatomy. The shine and dappling of the coat is the most positive key to indicate health.

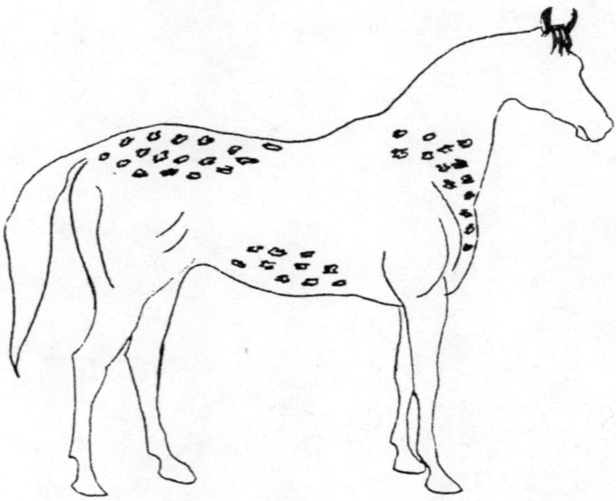

1—THE DAPPLED COAT—(positive)

Dappling is the light and dark spots that are in the skin of the horse, not in the hair. Dappling resembles large freckles. This type of coat indicates the horse is in excellent health and will appear on the horses particularly in the spring. Dappling cannot be groomed into the coat. It only appears when the horse has been fed and cared for properly. The checker-board often seen on the rump of the horse is NOT dappling. This is a grooming technique of beautification.

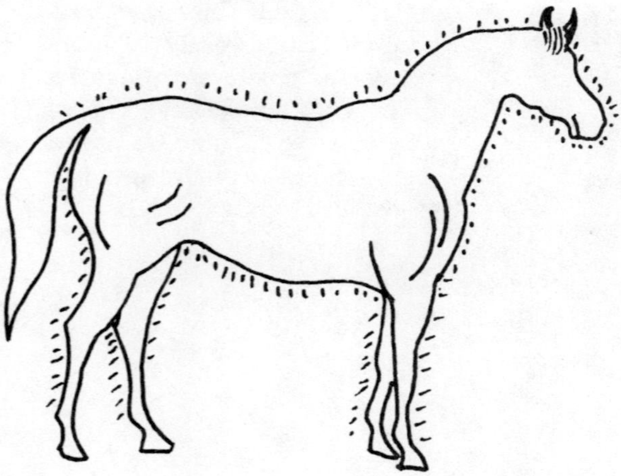

2—THE SHINY COAT—(positive)

This type of coat will reflect light and display such a gorgeous color it will be breathtaking. It looks like it has been highly polished for many hours. This also indicates good health and especially grooming.

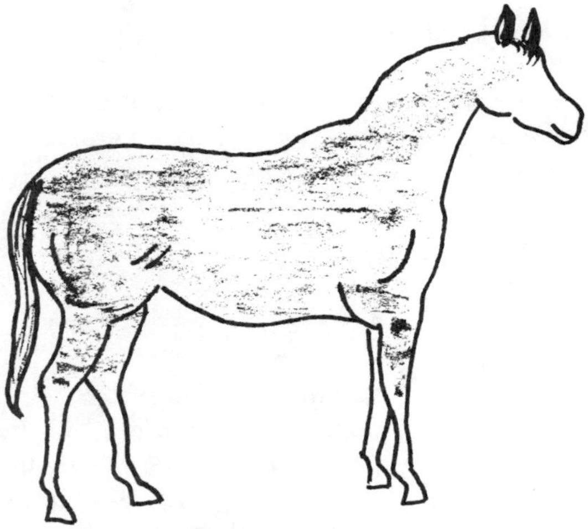

3–THE DULL COAT–(negative)

This type of coat will not reflect light; it will absorb it. Stomach hairs, looking uneven in length and scraggly, indicate excessive worms. The horse will be sickly, and will not run well.

4–THE WINTER COAT

This coat will look scruffy and definitely ungroomed. As nature permits, this coat will eventually disappear about March or April of each year. Depending on the time of year the horse is racing, I can't really type this coat as positive or negative. In California and Florida, winter coats may be limited to horses vanning from colder climates.

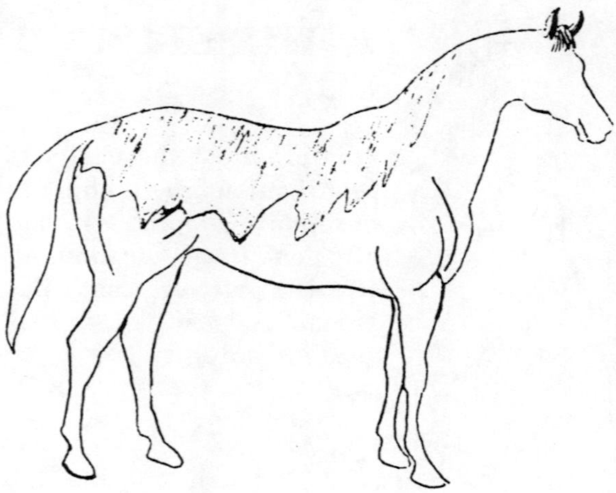

5–THE WET COAT

This coat is neither positive nor negative. The horse has been hosed down across his back or a bucket of water has been thrown over him. Do not mistake this for a washy coat. You'll be able to see a definite wet/dry line on each side of the horse.

6–THE WASHY COAT–(negative)

Horses often have a tendency to wash-out. This is a sweat condition that will first be seen on the neck and then will move across the body and finally drip under the belly. If the sweat is heavy it will turn to white foam if there is friction, such as reins rubbing on the neck, around the saddle and cinch area and between the rear thighs as the horse walks. The latter is often called kidney sweat. Kidney sweat alone would not be a negative, but if it is discolored the horse is either sick or is on some type of medication and would be a negative.

7—THE CLIPPED COAT

Part or all of the coat has been trimmed by a clipping machine. Clipping is usually done in the autumn, after the winter coat has grown. A positive sign of good grooming.

DAPPLED COAT

Curt Carlson

This is a perfect shot of a dappled coat. See how freckled the rump looks? Dappling will first appear on the rump and then gradually appear all over the body. The more dappling, the healthier the horse is. This is a positive sign.

NOT DAPPLED

Steve Stidham

Here it is, the famous checkerboard that everyone mistakes for dappling. This is not dappling. This checkerboard is created with a substance like Dippity-Doo. It's a gel like substance that is rubbed on the area that is to be groomed, then a comb is used to create whatever design desired. Very good looking, don't you think? A positive sign of good grooming.

SHINY COAT

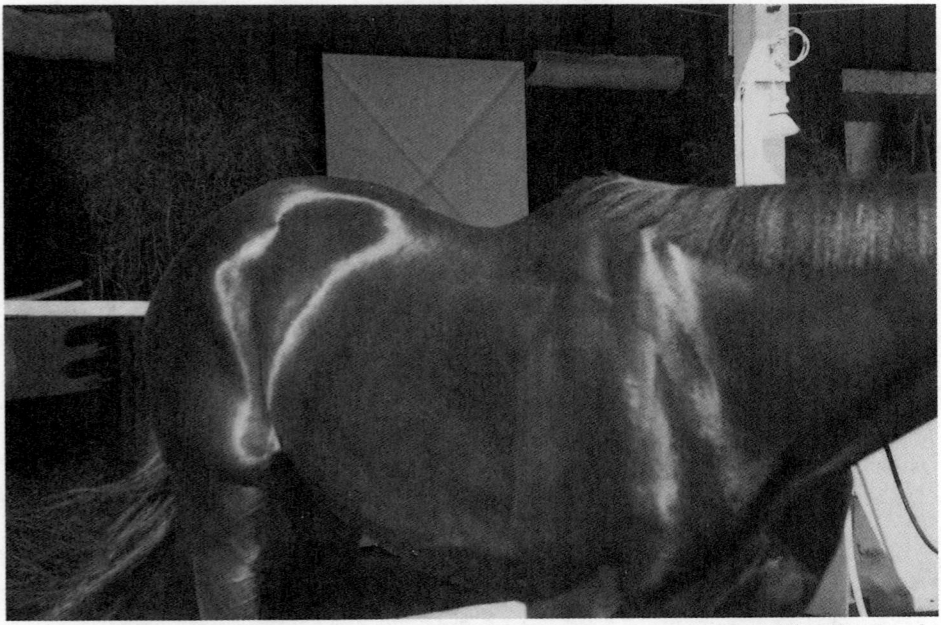

Millard Richards

I don't really think I need to explain this coat to you. I just wanted to point out that if you look closely you can see that the horse is dappled also. At least I can see it as I am writing this. This is a very positive sign. This coat is reflecting the sunlight tremendously. Good shot for a black and white one, huh?

WINTER COAT

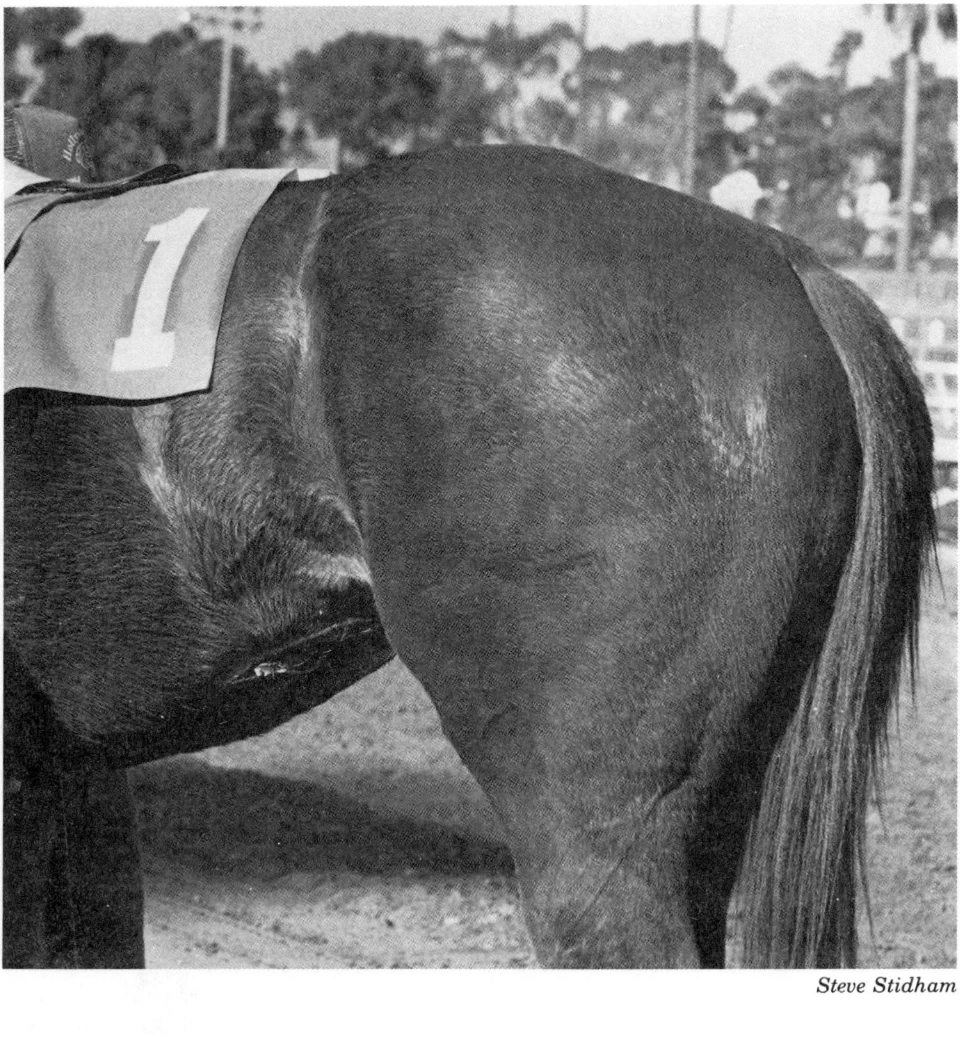

Steve Stidham

Yep, I got one of these too. This is the winter coat. Looks kind of scruffy, doesn't it? The lighter areas in the flank, looks like this horse has washed out a little. Seeing this wet look in the flank area prior to racing would be a negative. The scruffy coat alone is not. When spotting a scruffy coat, look for other positive signs such as muscle and attitude before accepting him as a win candidate.

THE TAIL

The tail of the horse is an indicator of how the horse feels. There are seven types that are easily spotted in the paddock, walking ring and post parade. There are two tail responses that can be spotted while the horse is racing.

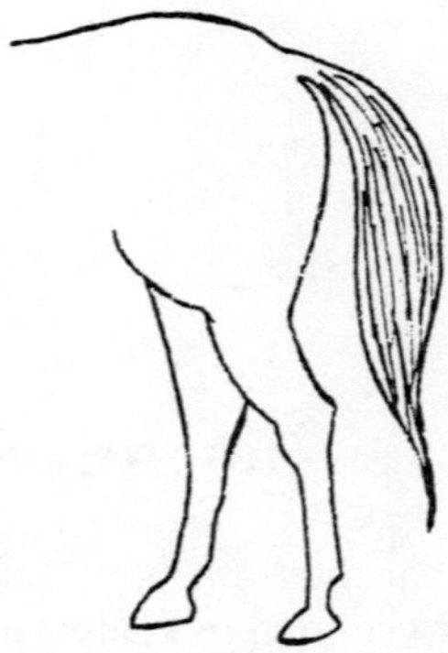

1–THE ARCHED TAIL–(positive)

The arched tail indicates pride and that he/she is feeling good. This horse will probably race very well. The tail will be arched so you'll be able to see daylight thru the base of the tail and the rear of the horse. The flag tail is similar to an arched one and is very positive. The tail will curve outward toward the horses backside, but then it will extend straight out. The tail hairs will drape like a flag.

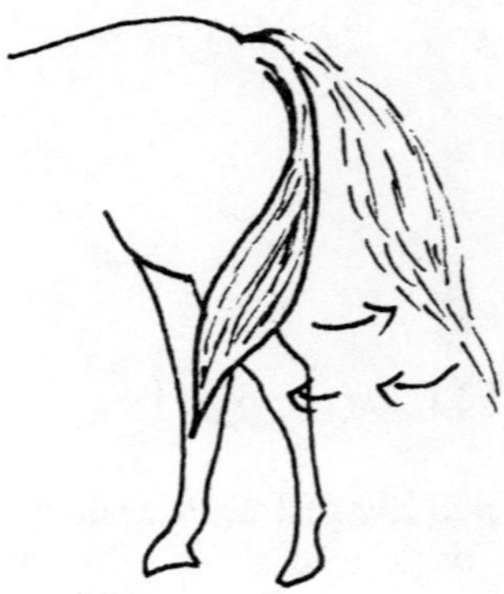

2–THE SWISHING ARCHED TAIL–(negative)

The arched tail that is swishing back and forth is a negative. The horse with this type of tail action is bothered by something and will not have his mind on racing. If the swishing arched tail is detected, and this particular horse is your handicapped choice, it would be wise to follow this horse with binoculars to the gate for often times the horse will calm down and the tail will stop swishing.

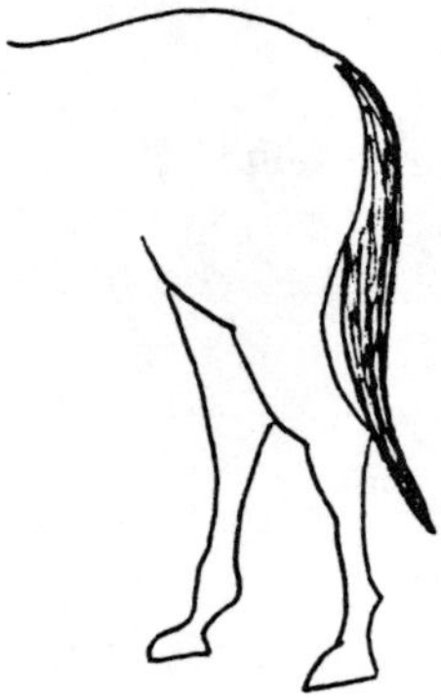

3–THE FLAT TAIL–(negative)

This tail lies very flat or loose to the rear of the horse. This indicates the horse really isn't feeling all that well. If a trainer were to grab the base of this flat tail and could pull it up, this horse would definitely be sick. On the other hand, if this horse were to snap his tail back down tight to his buttock the trainer would be reassured that his horse was O.K.

4–THE WORM TAIL–(negative)

This is a definite sign that the horse has or has had a bad case of worms. This condition occurs as the horse will back himself up against the back of his stall and rub his buttock back and forth. This causes the tail hairs to break at the base, or the tail may be rubbed hairless and raw.

5–THE MAD TAIL–(negative)

If the horse is mad he'll pop his tail up and down and swish it constantly back and forth. Please don't get close to a nervous horse, if his tail hits you it can really smart.

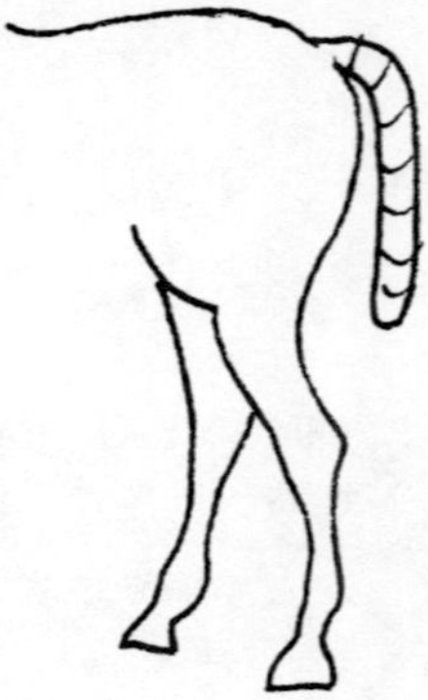

6–THE WRAPPED TAIL–(positive on off tracks)

Normally you will only see this type of tail on sloppy or muddy days. If the tail is not tied up before the race it will be laden with mud which will slow the horse down due to the slight increase in weight. Also true, once they are back from a race, mud will be switched all over themselves and everyone else that's close by. An "arched" wrapped tail during inclement weather is extremely positive.

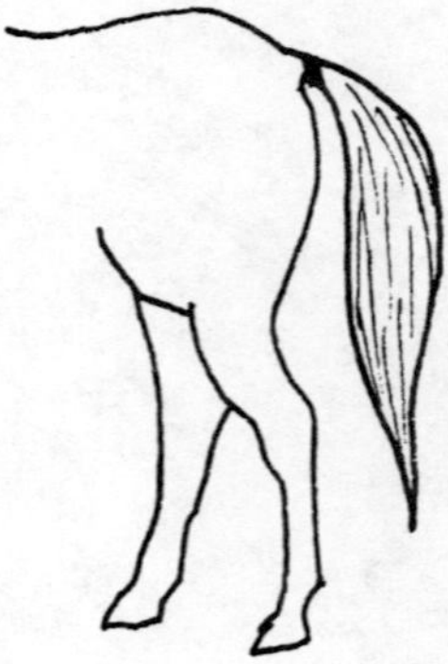

7–THE TIED TAIL–(negative)

At first glance, the viewer will think he/she is seeing an arched tail. But on looking closer, right at the base of the tail, one will see some form of tape or cord or rubber band so tight that it resembles a tourniquet. That is exactly what is intended. There is a difference in opinion, but there are trainers who believe that this effects the circulation system, and reduces the risk of "bleeding." In watching such horses run, it seems to me, that few are winners.

THE ARCHED TAIL

Curt Carlson

Look at the tail of this horse. See how nice and arched it is? If you look close, you'll see dappling on this winner also. The white area on the left foreleg is a Chestnut. It grows like a callous and is pared smooth. An arched tail is a positive sign.

THE FLAT TAIL

Curt Carlson

This horse definitely has a flat tail. See how tightly he has it clamped to his buttock. He obviously has some kind of problem and will not be in the winner's circle today. If this tail is observed, and it is one of your handicapped choices, one should follow this horse with binoculars to the gate for often times the horse will relax and the tail will arch eventually. Alcohol can be injected into the base of a nervous swishing tail and it will flatten. This method is used for show horses more so than Thoroughbreds.

THE FLAG TAIL

Millard Richards

This is a good shot of a flag tail. See how the tail hairs drop down from a more or less straight arched tail. It's hard to explain. How can a tail be arched and straight at the same time? Seeing is believing. Look at the restraint this exercise rider has on this horse. This little darling is telling the rider I feel good, I want to keep going. Many times you'll see an ad on television from a breeding farm and it will show a horse in the pasture displaying a very beautiful flag tail.

THE TAIL WHEN RACING

1—EXHAUSTION RESPONSE

As the horse is racing, particularly in the stretch drive home, often times you'll see the horse's tail pop up in the air. This is a sign the horse is tiring and is racing as hard as he/she can. This would be a horse I would hesitate playing next time out, especially if racing back in a higher class level or at a longer distance.

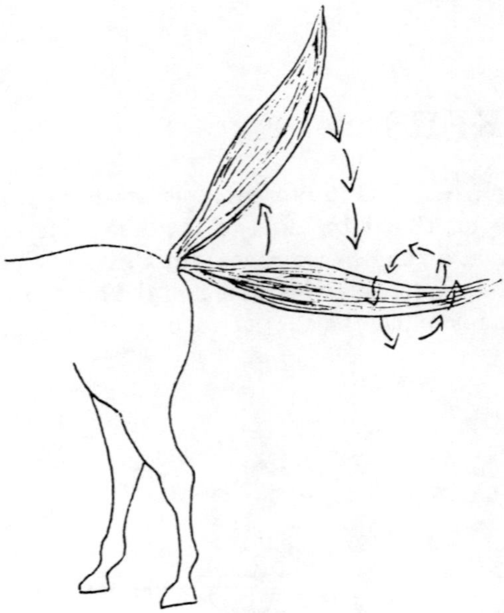

2—BUZZER RESPONSE

On occasion a horse's tail will pop up in the air and then start revolving in circles as he/she is racing. This is a sign that the jockey is packing a buzzer (electric device) and has zapped the horse with it. Granted this is extremely dangerous for the jockey to do and also illegal, but then again so is J-Walking. If you have placed a wager on another horse and the buzzed horse wins, just chalk it up to racing luck. Unfortunately, stewards and judges are not required to have special training in this country. Most do not know what to look for, or the meaning of what they see.

THE SHOES

There are nine or more different styles of shoes recommended to help the horse cope with varying track conditions.

Stickers, mud caulks, and block heels are special shoes normally worn to give traction on wet-weather surfaces. If the surface is wet, most tracks will identify which horses are wearing these shoes through a verbal announcement or through light identifications above or below the horse's number on the tote board. Some tracks hang up charts by the paddock showing you which type each horse in the race is wearing. Beware—even when the track is fast and/or on the turf courses, there are horses wearing these wet-weather special shoes, and they are winning. Especially stickers. There is proof of this on my video "Horses Talk: Where It Begins—The Early Years." Here we show close-ups of each type of shoe—with commentary.

The only shoes we will concern ourselves with are the shoes worn on the rear hooves.

Under the Rules of Racing, the Paddock Judge is only required to check the feet, and verify the type of shoe, when the track is "off."

On days when the track is fast, your eyes will be the only identifier of what types of shoes the horses are wearing. To do this, stand as close to the horse as you can, and fix your eyes on their REAR hooves. As the horse lifts up each rear hoof, you'll be able to spot the shoe type.

STICKERS

If a horse is wearing stickers, you will visually see shoes with metal caulks extending down from the shoe on the outer side of the heel. These sharp caulks extend down into the track as the horse races, thus giving the horse better traction. Just look for a shiny piece of pointed metal about the size of the first joint of your middle finger on the bottom of each shoe.

EXAMPLE:

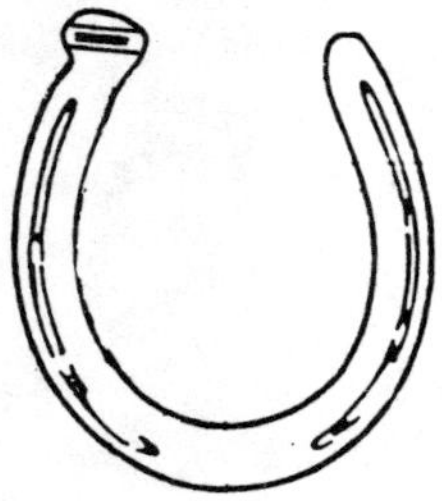

LEFT REAR

RIGHT REAR

SIDE VIEW

Many trainers run their horses with stickers on fast tracks and turf courses. If a horse who is wearing stickers, displays other positive physical signposts, I will always wager on him. (See Powerful Paddock Plays chapter for wagering strategy when more than one horse meets these criteria.)

MUD CAULKS

If a horse is wearing mud caulks, you'll see shoes with sharp caulkings on both open portions of the heel, plus a raised toe piece.

EXAMPLE:

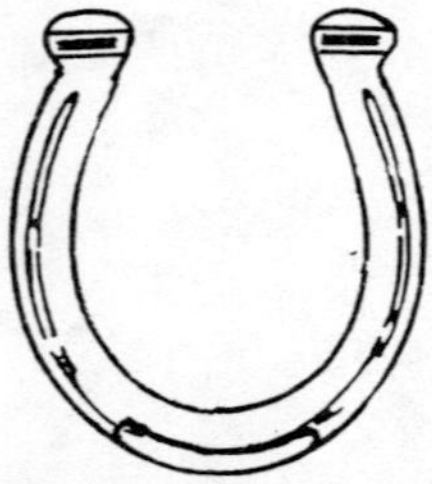

LEFT AND RIGHT SIDES LOOK THE SAME SIDE VIEW

Mud caulks are usually worn on off-track surfaces only. If your track identifies which horses are wearing mud caulks, be sure to double check that they are wearing them on the rear hooves. I've been to tracks where they do announce in advance what they are wearing, and I've gone to the paddock to check it out; some had them on their front hooves only, and some were without. Granted—all four hooves should be shod on off track days, and especially on the rear hooves, if they have any win intentions at all. Trainers really like to play games with the public. Again—there are certain breeds of horses that will win on off track surfaces without them. One should keep a record of those that do for future reference.

BLOCK HEELS

If a horse is wearing blocked heels, you will see a shoe with caulkings on both open portions of the heel of each hoof. The caulk looks like a small square of metal attached to the bottom of the racing plate.

EXAMPLE:

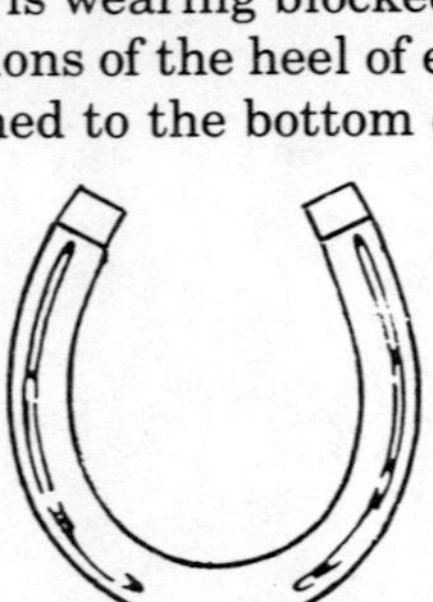

LEFT AND RIGHT SIDES LOOK THE SAME SIDE VIEW

This shoe is used to prevent horses from running down on their heels and to prevent slipping.

BAR SHOE

The bar shoe is a shoe that has a metal piece running across the open portion of the heel. This type of shoe is worn if there is a hoof problem, such as a quarter crack. It indicates they are trying to hold the horse's hoof together. I will not bet any horse that's wearing a bar shoe. Very seldom will you see them in the winner's circle.

EXAMPLE:

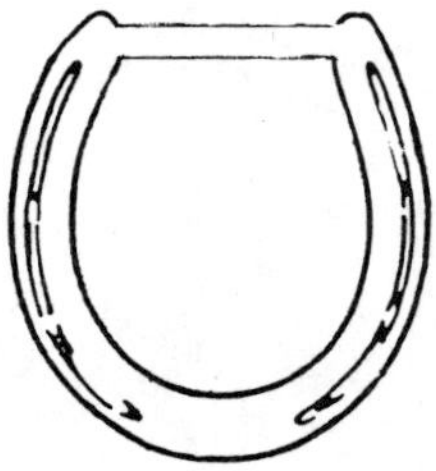

LEFT AND RIGHT SIDES LOOK THE SAME

If a horse is referred to as being slickshod this indicates he is wearing normal racing plates.

A STICKER

Curt Carlson

This is the shot of shots. Look at the right rear hoof of this Breeders Cup entry. Notice the shiny piece of metal. This is a sticker and no, this photo has not been re-touched. The patches noticed on the forelegs are interference patches. This horse obviously over-reaches and injures himself.

ANOTHER STICKER

Curt Carlson

I had another shot of a horse wearing stickers and I think it's important for you to visually see as many as possible so it'll be easier for you to spot them at the track. I've been told by a trainer that it's legal to wear stickers on the rear hooves, but not on the front ones. The right rear hoof displays a sticker, just barely visible. The right front hoof of this horse is slickshod.

SLICKSHOD

Curt Carlson

Here is a good shot of both front and rear hooves. They are slickshod. There is no caulking or metal extension visible.

IV.
MEDICATIONS

MEDICATIONS

The Thoroughbred, due to its unique body structure, and the impact of racing requirements through all types of weather conditions, often requires medication of some sort. They, like humans, will have the seasonal cold, influenza, and arthritic pains, (just to name a few), and will be treated accordingly.

Often, the Thoroughbred is forced to race with an "ouchy" condition, and is medicated to ease the discomfort.

The medications allowed in racing are controlled by each state.

The State Medication Rule Review compiled by the American Horse Council is printed periodically in the *Daily Racing Form.* This review indicates which states allow medications, the types, and the amounts permitted to be administered.

The three types of legal medications allowed prior to racing are: Non-steroidal anti-inflammatories (steroids are not legal), diuretics, and hormones.

The non-steroidal anti-inflammatory drugs allowed in several states consist of Butazolidin, (Phenylabutazone is the generic name for Butazolidin), Flunixin, Meclofenamic Acid, and Naproxen. These drugs are administered as pain killers (not as stimulants) for those horses afflicted with arthritis, sore feet, problems of hips and knees, etc.

With the medical experience I've had, I have learned that Butazolidin, (bute) does reduce inflammation, but does not heal the injury without proper rest. It also has a tendency to retain fluids in the body. Nothing overweight will run well. Keeping this in mind, any horse who is listed as being administered bute only, would be a very possible elimination as far as betting is concerned. At some tracks it is hard to find a listing of which horses are running on Butazolidin.

There is strong evidence to indicate that Butazolidin in the urine and in the blood can conceal illegal type drugs which could enhance or depress a horse's performance.

The legal diuretic drug used is Lasix. (Furosemide is the generic name for Lasix.) This drug is normally administered to "Bleeders." A bleeder is a horse that bleeds after or during a workout or race, due to ruptured blood vessels, usually in the lungs. Often, horses will discharge blood at the nostrils because of their long soft palate.

Once a horse has bled, he is put on the Vet's list and cannot be raced until removed, which is 10 to 14 days, depending on which state the horse is racing in.

When a horse is off the vet's list and able to race again, many trainers will have Lasix administered to help combat the bleeding problem. I've heard also from a pretty reliable source, that a certain herb administered to a horse will prevent it from bleeding.

Again, my medical experience has taught me that Lasix reduces fluids in the system and in no way could eliminate a nose bleed. It does lower the blood pressure through dehydration and this may help. If there is a respiratory hemorrhage, it could only mean that some sort of pulmonary disease exists.

For two consecutive years I have kept track of all bleeders at one particular track and these are the findings:

In 1984, 343 horses bled and landed on the Vet's list. 245 of those bleeders never reached the winner's circle. Of the 98 horses that made it, only 30 of those horses won more than once.

In 1985, 225 horses bled. 149 never reached the winner's circle and of the 76 that did, only 28 of them were winners more than once.

Combining the two years, 568 horses obviously had a pulmonary disorder, and had trainers smart enough to know that to continue racing them would kill them. Of the 174 horses that did reach the winner's circle, 75% won after being administered Lasix for the 1st time, indicating they weren't truly bleeders, but were administered Lasix to either dilute another drug or to race at a lighter weight. The other 25% won after receiving Lasix for the 2nd time.

In 1988, at the same track, of all horses going onto the Lasix list and continuing racing, only a handful hit the board during the balance of the race meet. Beware, also, of horses on Lasix when the weather is hot and humid. The combination creates too much loss of water and nutrients.

At some tracks, I have personally cashed many a ticket by playing those horses that race with Lasix for the first time, except for the fillies and mares. (The fillies and mares on Lasix just do not seem to have the strength like the males do. Very few hit the winner's circle on Lasix for the first time). To do this one must check the Vet's list each day for horses that have been listed as having bled. Keep a record of them, watch for them when they race back, and if medicated with Lasix, it would be a bet. For those of you that do not frequent your local track on a daily basis, I would suggest following those that are printed in the Official Rulings column of the *Daily Racing Form*. (Note: there are some tracks, however, where Lasix is a total negative, an automatic elimination).

Another winning Lasix situation to watch for are those horses that are shipped from states that do not allow Lasix, to states that do. For example: A horse shipping from Ak-Sar-Ben to Canterbury Downs, and is noted as using Lasix, could be an excellent bet.

Now, let's discuss exactly what Lasix does. Lasix, being a diuretic, will cause the horse to eliminate a great deal of water. Let's face it, anyone (especially humans,) feels better with a little weight off.

It has been said that Lasix dilutes other substances, and fooling the racing chemists seems to be the latest craze on the backside. Thank goodness though, with the new drug testing equipment they have, the crackdown is beginning. All ready we're seeing some trainers who thought they had a sure thing going, getting caught. Hopefully, soon, all shenanigans will cease.

Lasix binds itself to other drugs that may be circulating freely in the horse's system. Once the Lasix starts to work, all diluted drugs are then eliminated.

On the other hand, Lasix is very dangerous if not administered properly, especially in hot weather. It is an extremely potent diuretic and can cause kidney pain. If used over a long period of time, the horse should be monitored closely for any electrolyte deficiency, especially potassium, for without potassium one dies, and some horses do every year.

Now, I know you're thinking—if Lasix is so harmful, why are horsemen using it? They, like many of us, are from the old school, and hesitate to change or experiment with new ideas. Those that care are using a non-diuretic that is perfectly legal, and are getting the same results.

The drug Premarin (which is legally used in Colorado, Idaho, and Oregon) is a hormone. This drug stimulates the action of various organs. Horses suffering from too much racing are often given hormones to "get" one more race out of them. Likewise, horses who haven't been trained very much are given a hormone to improve their energy.

Let's discuss the horses that are on both Bute and Lasix. We know Bute retains fluid and Lasix gets rid of it. Here again, if Lasix was administered for the first or second time you can more or less expect a good race effort. However, in this case I normally rely more on what my eyes see in the paddock. If all signs are positive, it's a bet.

Those of you that are familiar with racing know that the urine of the winning horse is tested after each race. In some states, if any trace of medication is found in the urine, it represents a violation of the rules of racing and constitutes a fine or suspension of the trainer. In other states, a permitted level of certain types of medication is allowed, and if the urine tests in excess of that level, or if other medications other than allowable are found, again fines or suspension occur.

If one reads the Official Rulings printed in the *Daily Racing Form,* you will get a good grasp of what drugs are being used and who's getting caught. Like I said before, the crackdown is beginning.

Before I go any farther, let me state, "I am against racing any horse that has to have any type of medication."

O.K., so why is it happening, who is doing it, and what do we watch for?

All right, for the "WHY OF IT." You have a struggling trainer with a few horses; he hasn't had any of his charges in the money at all. How does he pay his feed bill, his grooms, the vet, the jockey? Yes, the owners are paying if he is a "public trainer," but they are also pressuring the trainer, threatening to switch to someone else. What's he to do? He's got a family to feed. He could quit all together, but horses may be all he knows.

In some cases, a trainer is located at a track where the winning purse levels are so low that even if his horse did win he couldn't survive. The business of racing is extremely expensive and sometimes not very rewarding.

In either of the above cases, the trainer takes a chance, enters his charge in an Exacta race, stimulates it, and instructs his jockey to bring his horse in second. The trainer then has someone wheel his horse second in the Exacta, 5 or 6 times. Possibly the jockey has the same number of tickets and they all rake in box car dollars. If the horse tests positive, the trainer knows he'll get fined. But by the time the test gets back he'll have already collected on his winning tickets and he has more than enough to pay the fine imposed.

WHO IS DOING IT? In some cases the trainer is. There are documented cases of trainers being caught with a tack room full of unlawful drugs and syringes. Then, again, the trainer could slip a little synthetic cocaine (undetectable through urine test) underneath a tongue-tie, and take his chances on his horse not racing himself to death, dying from a heart attack, or killing the jockey from the reaction.

In other instances, the veterinarian is doing it. Some have been charged with killing horses for insurance purposes. Some dope horses without the trainers knowing it, because they would rather cash a bet than anything else in the world. Who suffers besides the horse? The trainer; he's the one that takes the rap. Then, there's the old payola racket. You scratch my back, and I'll scratch yours.

O.K., we know what's going on; we're not stupid. We could say, "WE'RE MAD AS HELL, AND WE'RE NOT GOING TO TAKE IT ANYMORE." But who would care? We love racing, the exercise, the mental fatigue, the excitement from seeing our choice win, and yes, the cardiac arrests from seeing our choice lose. You have to love it, or you'd not be taking the time to read and study this course. Wanna bet?

Let's face it, some shenanigans are happening; they were happening way back when, and will continue to happen. Sure, we can fight them through legislation, and we will, but that takes time, and what's more important now is: "WHAT DO WE WATCH FOR?"

What's important, when viewing the horses, is to be aware of which ones have had a little help from their so called friends.

The ears of the horse will be the most visible signpost of a drugged horse.

If the ears are flopped sideways in the airplane position, the horse has been administered a (downer) depressant. Likewise, the eyes will be glazed and all movements of the horse will be poky. There will be no display of eagerness of any kind. The horse will appear as if he really doesn't care what's going on.

One would think a horse hit by a depressant would not race very well, but believe it or not, I have seen many airplaned ear horses win.

If the ears are frozen in one position, with no movement observed at all, the horse has been administered a (upper) stimulant. The eyes will bulge and will not focus properly. Usually, the horse will breathe erratically and will demonstrate spastic movements. His stimulated energy will become depleted either prior to the actual race, or while racing.

A horse over-stimulated with an upper could become dangerous to others while racing if not handled properly. A stimulant could also cause a horse to overly exert himself, causing his own injury. If you spot a horse with frozen ears, watch the trainers action after the race. The first thing he'll check is the horses legs.

The drugging of horses usually relates to lower class tracks, but sadly it is being seen more and more at major levels of racing.

V.
OFF-TRACK SURFACES

OFF-TRACK SURFACE CONDITIONS

Each track posts the surface conditions for the day's races on the Tote Board. Any condition labeled as good, slow, sloppy, heavy, muddy or frozen, due to inclement weather, is classified as an off-track.

The track surface varies (under any condition), between the inside along the rail, and the outside, toward the center of the track. Sometimes, along the rail, a cushion builds up and only those horses that are bred for stamina will win, because the going is deeper. Many times when the weather is really bad, mud puddles will form along the rail and the center of the track will be nice and dry.

If you are a true horse enthusiast and do not mind attending the races in the wind, rain, sleet, snow, and hail, I would suggest sitting through the first couple of races to first determine exactly what the track surface is like. Are the Clydesdales or Shetland ponies winning? Is it front speed or are the closers getting there first? Is the track in transition?

If the winner is a big horse or the Clydesdale, as I refer to it, and is not being challenged by a small horse, the track is obviously deep and only the strength and stamina of the Clydesdale can make it through. This often is true even when the track is posted fast, especially on the first race of the day and more so on the first race of the week.

If the small horse or Shetland pony wins and is not challenged by a Clydesdale, the track again may still be deep for the smaller horse lands easier and skims over the surface quickly.

If the Shetland pony and the Clydesdale are in the same race, you will often see them come in first and second. On these days, the typically sized Thoroughbred is disadvantaged.

If the front speed or just the speed horse of the race is winning, the track condition is probably labeled sloppy, thus indicating the bottom is still firm enough for the winner to grasp it.

If a closer wins the race, you can again expect the track to be fairly deep, for the closer has a heavier, more deliberate way of running.

If the track is changing from sloppy to good, or visa versa, I wouldn't even consider wagering. When in transition, it's a good day to curl up with a good mystery novel or love story.

The most preferable days to wager at any track are those that have been labeled fast or sloppy.

The majority of horses do not like the rain, and would much rather be in their stall or standing under their favorite tree.

One can visually tell if a horse will handle the off-track surface by watching him closely in the post parade. If the surface conditions do not feel secure to a horse, he will not have his mind on racing and will display his insecurity by picking up his rear hooves as high and as quickly as he possibly can as he canters. His muscles will be tense and his tail will be tightly clamped.

A horse who enjoys the wet surface will move calmly, with ears pricked forward and the closer together the rear hooves reach the surface, the better traction he'll have. If the horse happens to cross a puddle of water, he will actually look like he wants to stop and play in it. A horse displaying an arched tail with it wrapped for the off track conditions truly loves to race in the stuff.

Most horses will be shod with stickers or mud caulks, and that information is usually posted on off-track days. If posted as being shod with them, be sure to double check that they are being worn on their rear hooves.

The unwrapped tail and bandages would be negatives on off-track surfaces. Both will collect mud and add weight. High weights that are easily handled on a fast dry surface become impossible to carry on a deep track.

Horses with sore feet will often improve on softer tracks.

Any horse who has had the misfortune of falling due to wet weather conditions, will definitely remember the surface and may therefore have a tendency to pull himself up in the exact spot he fell, when raced again. Once a horse has fallen, the fear of doing it again will be instilled forever.

Many trainers are reluctant to race their horses in cold wet weather, and will either scratch them from the race or instruct their jockey to not pressure their mount at all.

On off-track days, a good place to stand and observe the horses is where they enter the track from the paddock and walking ring. This area is usually dry dirt, possibly with some sand or sawdust mixed in. When the horse first steps on the mud of the track surface, and it gives way beneath him, he will signal his distaste by angry movements of ears and tail. The horse that remains calm and unbothered, as entering the track itself, gives you a positive signal.

VI.
THE TWO YEAR OLDS

THE TWO YEAR OLDS

It seems extremely cruel to race the babies at two, for their bones are not fully developed and they are still so fragile. Many shin buck, or become bowed, due to racing them so young; but like us, they too have to earn their keep.

A two year old that has been whipped or manhandled, due to his normal high spirits, will not run well.

A youngster neighing while in the paddock is crying for his mother and has a strong desire to head back to the barn.

One that has stumbled out of the starting gate early in his career will usually become frightened of the gate and will remain so for several race starts, and may flatly refuse to enter it. If a flat refusal is noted at the starting gate, (no matter what the age) it is a definite negative.

Any display of a fast break out of the gate will have a distinct advantage, for many youngsters prefer following the leader.

A two year old that is well schooled will be calm and will stand still while being saddled. Being able to stand still is the most important lesson a youngster has to learn.

A two year old, being raced for the first time, who has three good works in the last 15 days printed in the *Daily Racing Form*, will be conditioned well and will display positive signposts in the paddock. If the total number of furlongs worked equals 14 or more, with one or two of the works from the gate, and the last work was three days prior to today's race, it's an automatic bet. Try this method; you'll surprise yourself at some of the enormous prices you'll pick up.

Be careful, though, many a workout for a horse has never reached *The Form* and some have been misrecorded. Accuracy varies between different geographical editions of the *Daily Racing Form*.

VII.
THE UNUSUAL AND TIDBITS

THE UNUSUAL AND TIDBITS

One afternoon my son and I had decided to go to the races. I had studied *The Form* the night before and felt confident about my selections.

We got to the track just in time to see the horses go parade to post in the second race. While standing at the rail, I noticed one horse that had a yellow "hue" all around his body. I first thought it was dust, but then after blinking my eyes, and looking again, I thought if it were dust, it surely wouldn't be under his belly. This yellow "hue" was across his back, down his legs, under the belly and on his neck. I couldn't believe my eyes, I'd never seen such a condition. I blinked my eyes again, and then asked my son to look at the number seven and tell me what he could see. He said, "the horse looks yellow to me, Mom; what's the matter with him?" I replied, "I don't know, but here's five dollars, go bet it to win." Sure enough he won and paid $17.20.

On another occasion, after the Handicapping Expo 83 Conference, I was at Santa Anita, viewing the horses in the paddock. I was discussing the horses with another conference participant and known handicapper, and I had given him my choice. He in turn looked at his *Racing Form* and stated, "that horse can't even get out of the gate, how could you possibly bet on him?" I stated, "the horse looks blue to me and I always bet on the unusual." Well, he thought I was crazy and believe me, I was beginning to think my eyes were failing me. But, just as the yellow horse I saw, this one was blue. It was a very cold windy day, so I thought to myself, maybe the horse was cold. Logical, but not a practical cause for a wager. I do have days where I'm not very practical, and that day was one, as I placed my bet on my blue horse.

The race was 9 furlongs and as the horses came out of the gate, sure enough, my blue horse was 8 lengths behind. I thought to myself, am I going to have to eat my words. As I stood watching my blue horse race alone, behind all the others, I was beginning to get very upset with myself. All of a sudden, off in the far turn, I noticed my choice beginning to pick up a little slack. He was now 7th, then 4th, then 2nd, and then they were in the home stretch. My stomach felt like it was stuck in my throat; he was catching the leader; I couldn't believe it, as he crossed the finish line 3 lengths ahead. He paid, $13.20.

Since then I have explained to several knowledgeable horsemen my visions, and asked if they knew what I was seeing. One told me that I obviously had the gift of seeing the winning aura of a horse. Horses have auras, just like people. Well, believe me, that answer didn't satisfy me at all, for if it were true, I'd have seen others, and I haven't.

Another told me that when furriers buy pelts, they look for the tiny guard hairs that stand up above the actual fur. These guard hairs indicate the animal was in his peak season. Likewise, that's what I was seeing on each of the yellow and blue horses, their guard hairs and they too were in their peak season. This explanation sounds more logical to me.

I keep recalling from my memory banks, tidbits that I've failed to incorporate in the main body of this course, so this section is devoted to them.

As we grow older, we become senior citizens; likewise with horses, they too become seniors. Often, a race will be written for a certain age and will include the seniors. It's at this time you'll occasionally see the oldest horse win. Not only do the older horses have more racing experience, but they also have the respect of the younger horses racing with them. The younger horses often will not pass the seniors.

If this sounds like a wild or weird statement, the reader should know that Thoroughbreds, like some other species, show a phenomenon called "pecking order." Usually this is taught them by their mother.

If you go to a breeding farm, watch the mares and foals in the pasture. One mare will always be first to the water trough or the feed bin. Another will be constantly second, and others will follow in clusters.

The "pecking order" is often involved in those horses seen in the *Daily Racing Form* with many seconds and thirds, but no wins.

Much can be learned by studying the past performances printed in the *Daily Racing Form*. For example: a horse whose performance indicates he lugged in or out in his last few races indicates the horse is sore. If a horse lugs out, or to the right, it indicates he is suffering with pain somewhere on his left side. Likewise, if he lugs in, he is enduring pain on the right side.

A horse who fell on his last start should be disregarded altogether, until he proves he is sound by displaying a good race effort.

Horses whose past performances indicate they were eased in their last start, could be the cause of several things and not always a problem. The horse could have disliked the surface condition and the jockey could feel he was losing his footing so he just eased him. On the other hand, the trainer could have instructed the jockey to ease the horse, so the odds would be higher the next time he raced. I have seen many horses win, after being eased in their last race.

Let's discuss quickly a horse who is walking in the paddock and occasionally snorts. This horse is not clearing his nostrils. He is letting the other horses know that he intends to be the winner. It is his day, and under no circumstances are you to get in his way. This is a powerful play and the horse is actually talking to you.

Those of you that are speed handicappers, beware. The official timing of each race does not start when the starting gate opens. In fact, at the majority of the tracks, the horses race 10 lengths, or two full seconds before the official timing begins. Each track timing is different, as well as at each distance. For instance, a horse racing eight furlongs at Santa Anita races four full seconds before the timer starts, while at Hollywood, at the same distance, he'll only race two seconds. A great deal of energy is exerted in that period of time, know what I mean?

The following, is a chart of the different distances and time differences I've tracked so far.

DIRT TRACKS	6F	6.5F	7F	8F	1.70	8.5F	9F	9.5F	10F
Aqueduct	2.1		2.1	2.3		2.1	2.4		
Arlington	1.2		1.4	1.3			3.1	2.3	
Bay Meadows	1.1								
Belmont	2.1		2.2						2.2
Del Mar	2.1			4.0		2.3			
Garden State	2.1			2.0	1.3	2.0			1.2
Golden Gate	2.2			4.3		3.2	2.4		2.1
Hawthorne	2.1				2.1	3.2			
Hialeah	2.3		1.0			3.2	4.3		
Hollywood	2.0		2.0	2.0			2.2		
Laurel	2.1			2.1			2.0		1.4
Longacres	2.3	2.3		4.3		2.3			
Meadowlands	1.4				2.0	2.0	2.0		
Philadelphia	2.1								
Pimlico	0.1					2.2			
Santa Anita	2.4	2.4		4.0		2.4			2.1
Saratoga	2.4		2.2				2.0		

VIII.
BEFORE THE RACES

BEFORE THE RACES

At the track there are three areas where you can relate flesh and figures. The paddock, walking ring and post parade. Any horse that figures to be a winner on paper should be reinforced with positive physical signposts from each of these areas. If it doesn't, you should either eliminate it, and upgrade your second choice, or pass the race entirely. If you are viewing a race of nothing but first time starters, then each horse should be treated on an individual basis.

The pre-requisite to this course is a good set of eyes and a good pair of walking shoes.

Get to the track early. Try to arrive at least one hour before the races start. Purchase a program. This program will be your guide to winning the rest of the day. Hopefully, you've already purchased the *Daily Racing Form* and have handicapped your day's selections. If you haven't, and you know nothing of handicapping then don't expect to win as often as those that do. However, after learning the positive signposts you'll be able to hit some nice longshots. I do suggest that you learn at least basic handicapping to assist in building your bankroll.

Locate a seat that's fairly close to the paddock so you won't have to walk yourself to death. This I know is difficult at many tracks. At some tracks I've been to, I've threatened to wear my roller skates, but as of this date I haven't had the guts to do so. Sit down and relax now, as when the races start there won't be much time for that. As you are relaxing, take your *Racing Form* and transfer your day's selections for each race from it to the day's program. Use a blue felt pen to do your markings. It's easy to review when through and not much pressure is required to make a mark. From experience, however, I do suggest if it's raining to switch to a ball point pen. Otherwise, you'll have a smeared mess. Enter your top three selections with their appropriate number and a circle around it. Enter it where the morning line odds are printed for each horse. Use this area, for it's about the only portion of the program we won't be writing on.

EXAMPLE:

8 | HILLTOP FARM (Edgar Lambert) Gray, Black "HF" White Cap | JESSE CAUDILL | (1) 4
DROSERA B **118** | **EDDIE DELAHOUSSAYE** (Post Pos. 8)
B.f.(1983), Dewan—La Croix

Now, (you've rested enough) locate the medication list. Usually, this is posted at several locations for the public to view. I say "usually," for some tracks post it only in one area, and others don't post it at all. If you are not already aware of where it's posted—please ask someone. The medications list is a list of all horses that will be administered some type of medication prior to the race. Transfer the medication list to your program. Record a capital "L," (Lasix) "B," (Bute) or both with a circle around them just above the horse's name. If every horse is medicated in the race just write "ALL" at the top of your program for that race. Many tracks are now listing the medications in their programs.

EXAMPLE:

7 | GLENCREST FARM (John and David Greathouse, Sr. and Jr.) Gold, Green Hoops, Green Bars on Sleeves, Green Cap | GEORGE R. ARNOLD II | 3
(L) **TRICKY FINGERS** B **118** | **PAT DAY** (Post Pos. 6)
B.f.(1983), Clever Trick—Finger Ring

Your next project is to locate where the shoe board is. Knowing what type of shoes the horse is wearing is extremely important, but you'll only be able to mark on your program the types of shoes just before each race. This cannot be done in advance like the medication list. Again, many tracks do not have shoe boards, and in this case you'll have to use your eyes before each race. Often, it's nothing but a board of lights—different colored lights. Each color represents a different type of shoe. It will be easy to understand if you can find it. If the shoe board is in the paddock, the lights should be on for the first race. If so, on your program where the number of each horse is printed record the type of shoe. Use a capital "S" if the horse is wearing stickers, a capital "MC" if the horse is wearing mud caulks, a capital "BS" if the horse is wearing a bar shoe, and a capital "B" if the horse is wearing blocked heels. There are other types of shoes, but the ones I have just listed are the important ones. If the horse isn't wearing a modified shoe, as listed above, he is classified as being "slickshod." If so just draw a diagonal line through the horse's number on your program.

EXAMPLE:

5S | EVERGREEN FARMS (C. N. Ray) Light Blue, Green Evergreens, Green Sleeves, Light Blue and Green Cap | TED McCLAIN | 15
GREAT REEF **112** | **JULIO ESPINOZA**
B.c.(1982), Grundy—Belle Reef

At many tracks, you'll be able to visually view the Thoroughbreds walk from the barn to the paddock. The only racing equipment you'll see being worn by the horse during this walk is the bridle, blinkers (sometimes), and leg wraps (bandages). All other equipment will be added or removed while the horse is in the paddock.

Some trainers will have blankets on their horses for protection against the cold, rain, light, and flies.

If the track is muddy, you'll see most all horses with their tails tied or braided. This is done to prevent the tail from picking up mud and adding extra weight.

LEG BANDAGES

The leg bandages usually seen are white heavy flannel or woven elastic. Large front and rear bandages are usually worn to support a tendon that may not be sound, or as a precaution to prevent the horse from striking himself. Often, large front leg wraps are "cold-water bandages." These bandages are designed to hold a quantity of water and assist in cooling out a fevered leg as long as possible. They are removed from the leg prior to racing. I normally disregard any horse wearing this type of bandage.

The smaller bandages on the rear hooves are called rundowns and are used to support the pasterns. They are worn to prevent the heel from striking the track too hard, thus causing an injury. I have seen horses enter the paddock wearing rundowns that have had spots of red color on them to indicate blood. This is nothing more than a trainer manipulation to throw the public off the horse. If the horse was truly bleeding the track veterinarian would scratch the horse from the race entirely.

If the track is muddy, any bandages will add extra weight and if my handicapped choice for the race is wearing them it's normally a no bet situation.

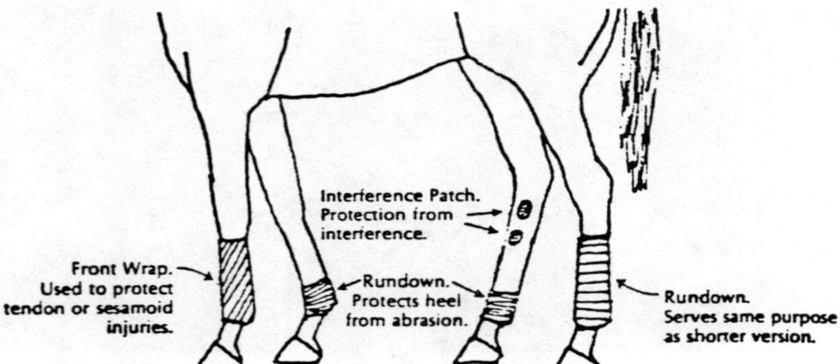

LEG WRAPS

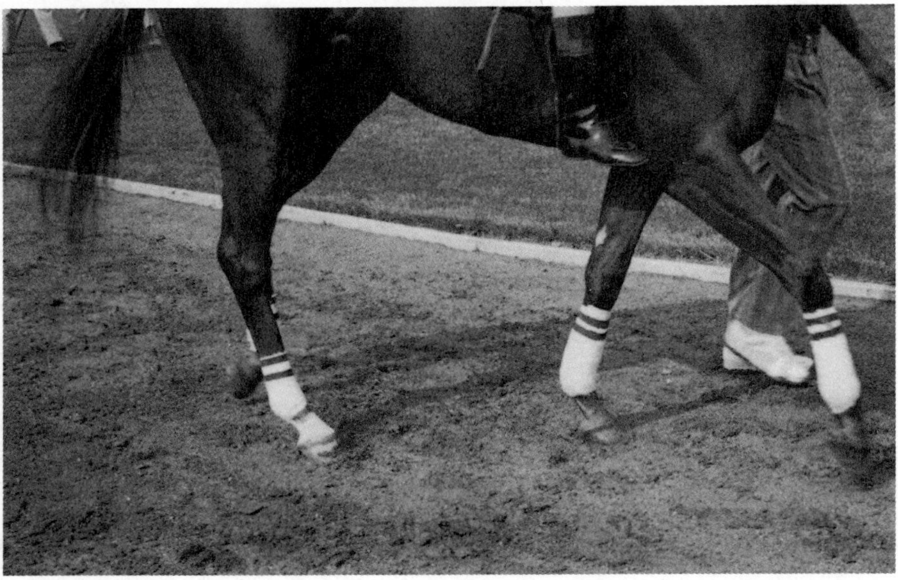

Curt Carlson

Front and rear legs are wrapped. Front wraps are too bulgy for me to wager on this horse.

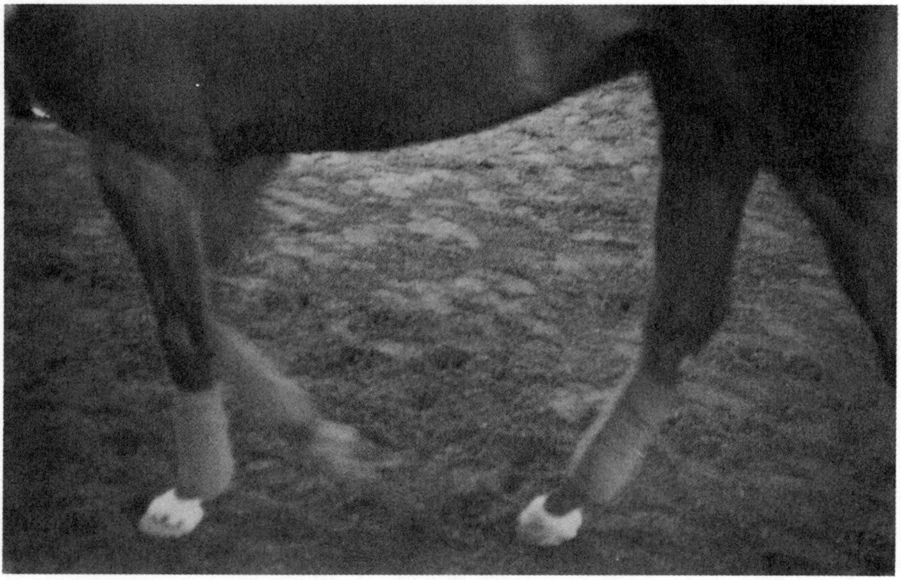

Curt Carlson

Elastic bandages worn here will probably be removed before racing.

MORE WRAPS

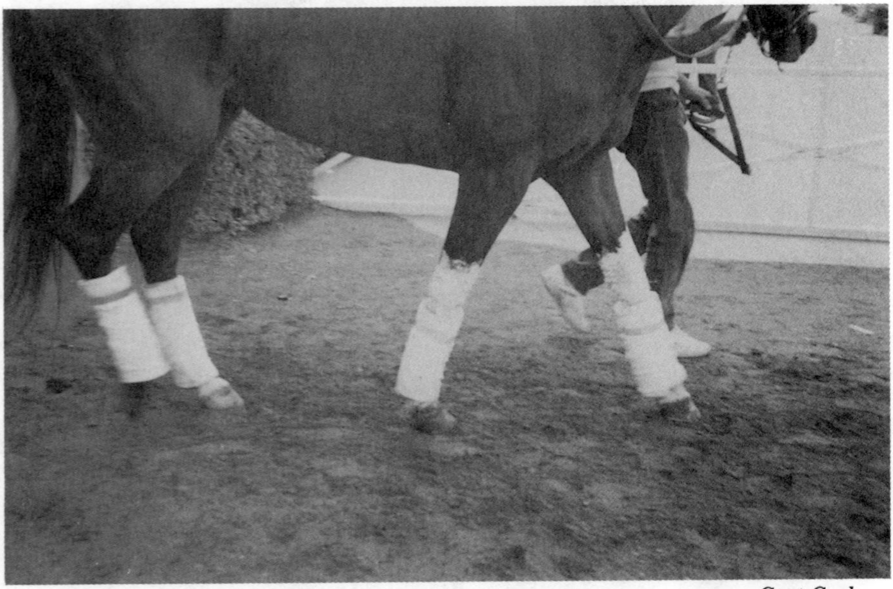

Curt Carlson

This horse has a real problem. Note medication on the front legs. Leg wraps such as these are often seen worn by schoolers.

Steve Stidham

These are cold water bandages which are used for cooling the legs and protection.

"RUNDOWNS"

Steve Stidham

This picture shows clearly the meaning of "rundown bandages." Imagine this horse's ankles if not protected by the bandaging. A combination of conformation and running action caused this horse's sesamoids to hit the ground with every stride.

BLINKERS

The colorful blinkers you'll see being worn by the Thoroughbred will vary in size; half cup, three-quarter cup, full cup and will be worn on either one or both eyes. They are worn to prevent distractions. If a trainer puts blinkers on or takes them off of his horse, he must get official permission before he enters the race. This information is printed at the bottom of the racing program, or announced prior to each race. What is important to note is, if the horse is wearing blinkers for the first time, watch the horse's head. If he's throwing his head around, he is probably having trouble adjusting to them and will not have his mind on racing. Blinkers should never be worn by a horse unless they improve his running. Many horses will win with blinkers on and lose with them off.

I know of a trainer who used to manipulate his horse very well with blinkers. He had discovered that when his horse raced, if any horse tried to pass him, his horse would instinctively exert himself that much harder. The trainer put blinkers on his horse, probably as a precautionary method, to prevent the horse from racing himself to death. Then, one day I noticed the blinkers he had put on, had small slits on each side of the cup. The slits were just large enough for the horse to see another coming up along side of him. Sure enough he won. The trainer obviously didn't want to declare officially that he was removing the blinkers so he just rigged up another pair with slits. His horse won every time he put on blinkers with slits, and lost with blinkers with no slits.

BLINKERS

Steve Stidham

This is a good shot of a horse wearing blinkers. Their purpose is to assist the horse in focusing his attention forward. The white blinker cup is called a semi-cup, which gives the horse more forward vision and a little side vision. The blinker cups come in different sizes and colors. A cup which covers the entire eye is called a goggle. Goggles will be used to protect an injured eye but not in off-track weather conditions.

SLOTTED BLINKERS

Curt Carlson

The blinker cup visible here has a slot cut in the back portion of it. Can you see it? This hole was put there by the trainer. He obviously doesn't want the horse to see what's beside him, but he does want him to see what's coming behind him.

BRIDLES

The bridles worn by the Thoroughbred varies. Most all racing bridles consist of a headpiece and throat-latch, a browband, noseband, cheekpieces and reins.

A horse's mouth is as sensitive as our own. Care must be taken not to injure the parts of the mouth and head that come in contact with the bit and bridle. A bridle too tight causes a horse to toss his head, while one too loose may cause a horse to put his tongue over the bit.

Some bridles will criss cross, and it looks like a figure-eight going across the horses face. This figure-eight noseband is used to keep the horses mouth shut.

Another device seen is one SEATTLE SLEW wore. It looks like an inverted "Y" on the face of the horse. This device is named the "Sure Win" bit holder. This bridle can be adjusted to keep the bit on the roof of the mouth, thus making it difficult for the horse to get his tongue over it.

BITS

To get the best out of a horse the proper bit should be used. There are several varieties and shapes.

Since we, the handicappers, will not be able to see inside the mouth of the horse, we will only concern ourselves with what's on the outside and its effect on racing.

The standard race bit which most trainers start their horses on is the Dee-Cheek Race Snaffle or D-Bit. When this bit is used the handicapper will see a "D" shaped metal piece on each side of the horses mouth, which the reins are attached to.

A horse that has a problem of running sideways, away from the rail on a turn, will probably be wearing a Dexter Snaffle Ring, or more commonly known as just a ring bit. You'll see a large ring that goes through the mouth and under the jaw. The ring creates pressure against the jaw as well as the cheek when tension is applied to the reins.

The horse that lugs in or out, will probably be wearing a Slide Bit. This bit can be easily spotted, for it extends outward away from the face about an inch or so on both sides. It is a hollow bit with a rod running through it. The rod is about 3 inches longer than the hollow bit and the reins are attached to the rings attached to the rod. This bit gives additional leverage against the horse's mouth.

If a horse tends to lug out, when the jockey tugs at the left rein to keep him in, the rod will slide to the left extending outward to the left. This creates much more leverage for the jockey, and allows better control. If the horse tends to lug in, then the jockey produces the same result when pulling on the right rein.

For horses that are hard to control there is another type called a "cage bit." On one side of the bit, there is a round piece of metal with dozens of small prongs. The prongs are square at the end.

When this bit is put on the horse, all these prongs are inset, inside the circular metal enclosure we can see from the outside. But if the horse fights the jockey trying to lug out, a sharp tug on the reins will cause these prongs to pop out, striking the horse's tender mouth. The horse will respond to this and move away from the pressure.

If the horse is one who tends to lug in, then the bit will be reversed when the equipment is put on, and the "cage" will be on the left.

The cage bit and the slide bit (sometimes called "ride-out bit") are not seen often, but can be a good "angle play." I see horses that are virtually never worse than second when wearing one of these two bits, and down the track without them. This is another case where trainers can manipulate running style, and what will appear in the *Daily Racing Form* past performances.

SHADOW ROLL

The shadow roll often worn by horses usually consists of a light-weight fleecy lamb's wool, circular, two or three inches diagonally, that is attached to the bridle and fits under the eyes. It is used to prevent a horse from seeing and reacting to his own shadow. Sometimes the shadow roll is used to keep the horse's head down, where otherwise the head is too high, interfering with the horse's best "action."

I'm sure by now, you're aware that I'm trying to give you a detailed description of the equipment you'll see as the horses enter the paddock. All items mentioned have their purpose and are important, but for the sake of keeping this course as simple as possible, I'll only have you record on your program, the more important positive signposts.

Now, rush over to the paddock, find a good place to stand, and let's begin.

WHAT'S WHAT

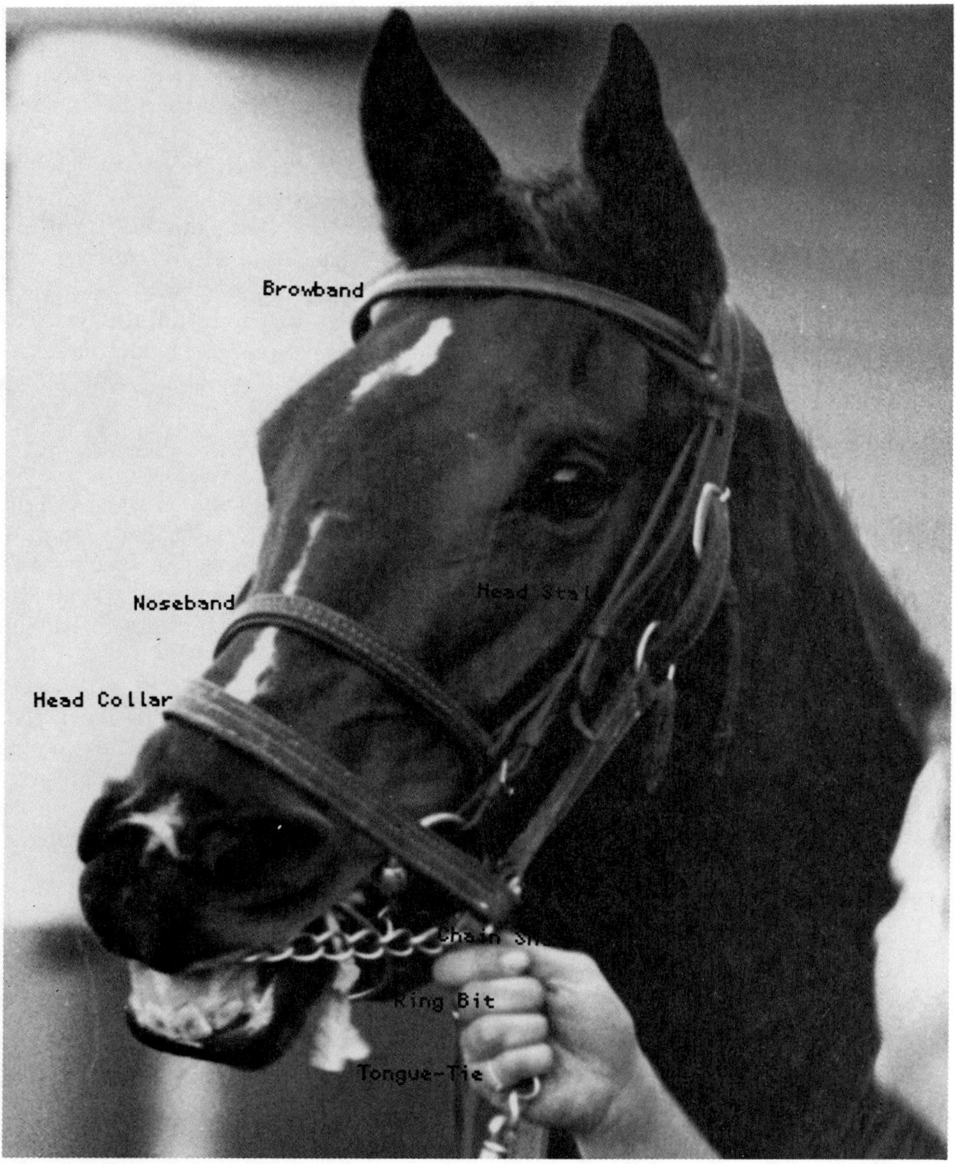

Steve Stidham

O.K., just exactly what is what? Well, we have the browband, the noseband, the head stall, the ring bit, the tongue-tie and the head collar with the chain shank. You got it? Sure you do. Just in case, I'll point them out above.

FIGURE EIGHT

Steve Stidham

Across the bridge of this horse's nose, you'll see two criss-crossing leather straps. This is the figure eight noseband. This piece of equipment helps to keep the horse's mouth from moving side-to-side. We can also see the tongue-tie, and the ring bit.

SHUR WIN BIT HOLDER

Steve Stidham

This is a side view of the Shur Win or Sure Win bit holder. It seems to hold the bit more up towards the roof of the mouth. SEATTLE SLEW won many a race with this bit holder on.

"D" BIT

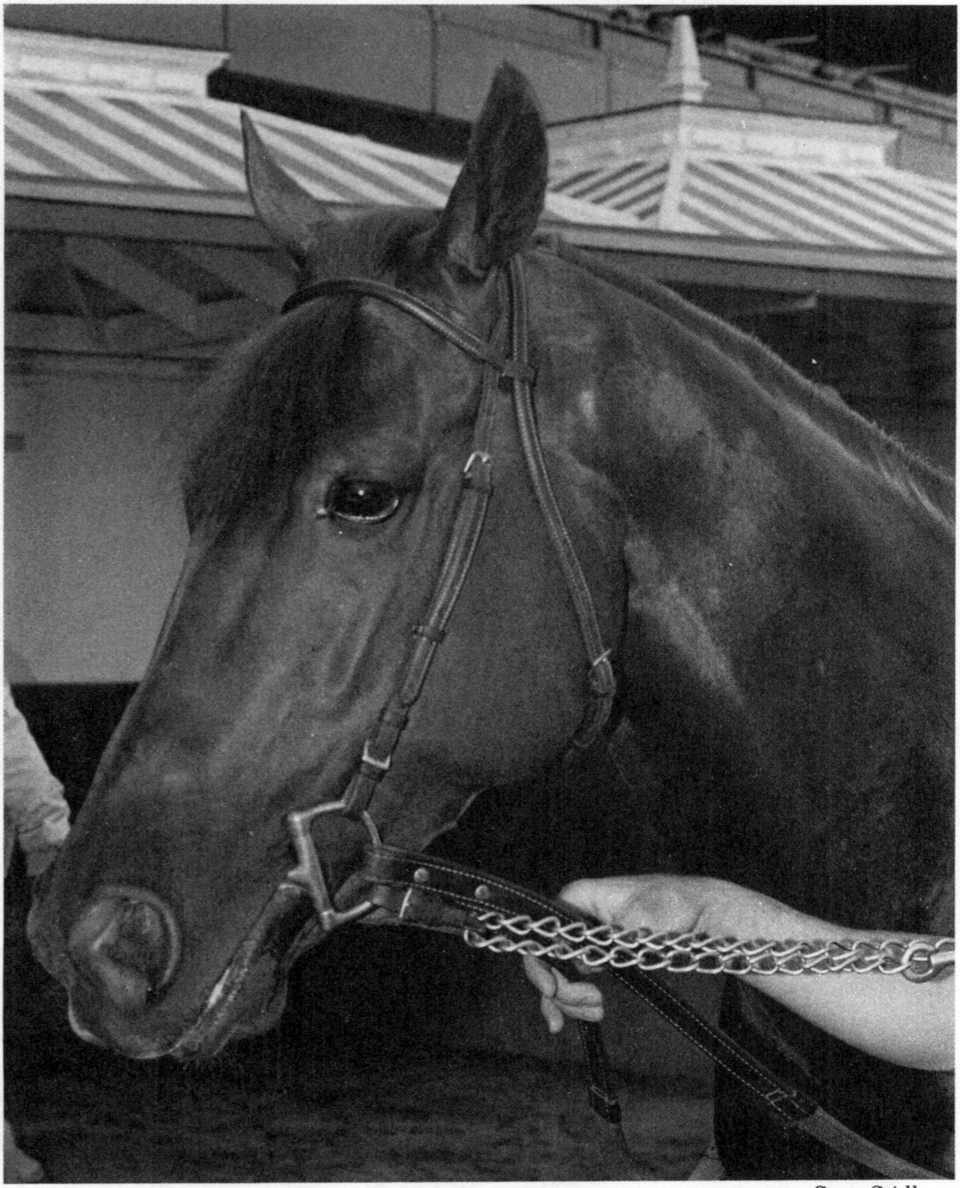

Steve Stidham

This shot shows the "D" Bit. See the "D" piece of metal the headstall and reins are attached to. The handler controlling this horse has the chain shank looped through the chin strap. Seems to me that is where the chain shank should be all the time.

RUBBER "D" BIT

Steve Stidham

The bit this horse is wearing is the Rubber "D" bit. The piece going through the horse's mouth is made of rubber. This is usually used on a horse whose mouth is pretty tender. I wouldn't think trainer intent would be too high with a horse wearing this type of bit.

RING BIT

Steve Stidham

This is a pretty good shot of the "Ring" bit. See the metal ring going thru the mouth and under the chin. This bit is used for horses that need to have just a wee-bit of coaxing to stay in line. This bit usually has metal cheek prongs attached, but I don't seem to spot them with this one. See how neatly the head collar is holding back the reins. The head collar will be removed before racing.

SHADOW ROLL

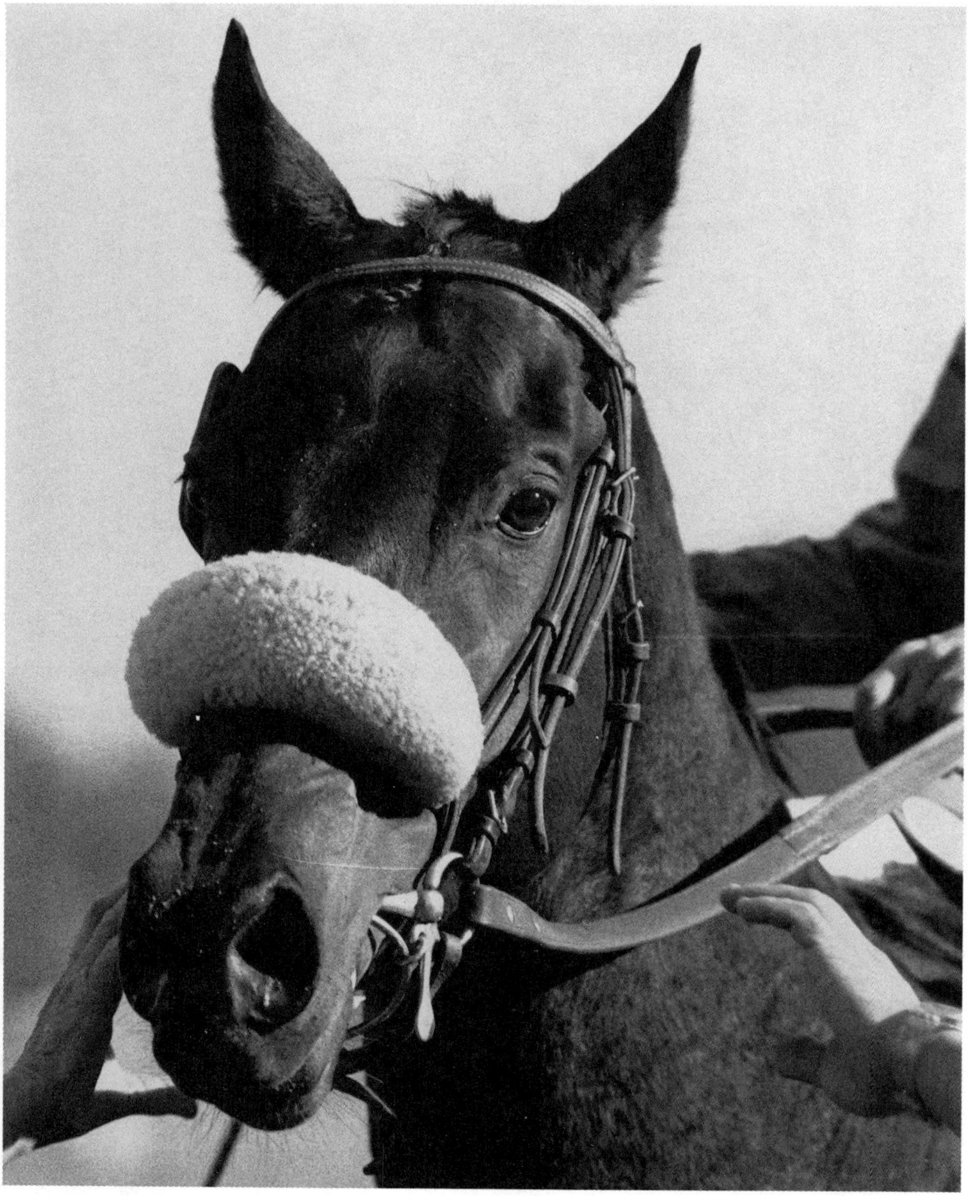

Steve Stidham

The white fuzzy thing sitting on the bridge of this horse's nose is called a shadow roll. This horse also is wearing a ring bit. Can you see the ring going under his chin?

IX.
THE PADDOCK

THE PADDOCK

In any of the pre-race areas in which you are able to view the horses, remember they will not stand still for you to make your notes. You have to train your eyes to be quick, as well as your fingers.

The paddock is an area next to the track or grandstand where the horses are saddled prior to the race. The horses will be led into this area (usually in number order) by their groom, (handler) and/or their trainer. Their main purpose is to keep their charges as comfortable and calm as possible until race time. Some horses will be led directly to their numbered stalls and others will be walked around. It's in this area I stand first with my program in hand and begin my recordings of what I see. It's much easier if two people work together. One could softly speak what he sees ("Number one, nice shine, number two, dappled," etc.) and the other could write the information he is hearing on the program.

The following program markings are suggested abbreviations only, to eliminate the full writing out of each signpost.

As the horse enters the paddock, and if he's on his toes, (prancing) mark on your program a capital "T," (meaning on his toes.) He will be on his toes constantly, even before he's mounted.

EXAMPLE:

5 | KENNETH BURKHART — OWNER
Green, White "AF," White Sleeves
White Cap
PUT HER ON ICE B **121**
Dk.b. or br.f.(1983), It's Freezing—Snap Crackle n Pop

20
SCOTT MILLER
(Post Pos. 4)

This indicates the horse is feeling good. A horse will prance voluntar. and will do it because he wants to, not because he has to. The more a hor prances the better he feels. Many horses will prance a little, then walk a litt! This signifies the horse feels O.K., but is not as perky as one who is on his to constantly. An O.K. horse will win, and probably there won't be any oth horse in the race that will look any better.

I have found "on its toes" to be the most important sign in Quart Horse racing. At Los Alamitos, boxing the 2-3 horses on their toes brings many an exacta. And if the horse stays on its toes through the post parade, it is a strong "win bet."

There are times you'll see a handler parade a prancing "Schooler" around the paddock or stand with him quietly in a stall. This is a horse that's going to school just like you and I did. He is getting familiar with the crowd noises and excitement of pre-race preparations, but will not be racing. Usually, a schooler can be identified by the large protective front and rear leg wraps he'll be wearing.

Next, note the coat of the horse. look for the EXTREMELY shiny coats and coats that are dappled. Dappling resembles large freckles. It is the light and dark spots that are in the skin of the horse, not in the hair. If a horse's coat is shiny, record a capital "NS"—meaning nice shine. If it's dappled, record a capital "DAP." If the coat of the horse shows neither of the above leave your program blank for that horse.

EXAMPLE:

4	ARPARK STABLE JOSEPH M. BOLLERO (Ralph Ross, et al) Orange, Gray Cross Sashes, Gray Cap **JET SET PEG** DAP **118** B.f.(1983), Tri Jet—Peggy's Cove	**15** **EARLIE FIRES** (Post Pos. 3)

An unruly horse will often injure himself in his stall creating a flesh wound. A flesh wound on a horse, when healed, will turn white. Often you'll see a healed flesh wound covered with shoe polish to match the coloring of the coat of the horse.

Fix your eyes on the legs of each horse. Start with the front legs, then to the rear. Take particular note of any horse with large front bandages that are bulging.

If firing of the leg has occurred, that portion which has been fired is usually sheared or shaved. It will look like a series of small holes have been punctured through the skin.

Either of the above conditions indicates a definite leg problem, so disregard the horse altogether. If noted, just draw a line through the horse's name.

EXAMPLE:

3	MRS. AND MRS. EUGENE V. KLEIN D. WAYNE LUKAS Gold, White, Blue and Gold Lightning Bolt, White, Blue and Gold Lightning Bolt on Sleeves, Gold Cap ~~**JOY TO RAISE**~~ b **121** Dk.b. or br.f.(1983), Old Faithful—Joy To Tell	**4** **JORGE VELASQUEZ** (Post Pos. 2)

By this time the horses are now pretty much in their stalls and are being saddled. Watch closely at this point as to what is going on, such as a horse who is putting up a fight while being saddled, kicking stall walls, etc. Mark your program with a capital "F." This horse is frightened or fractious, and is expending a lot of energy. He will not have his mind on racing; a definite negative.

EXAMPLE:

2 | SPENDTHRIFT FARM — ELMER S. LITTRELL
(Leslie Combs II, et al)
Orange, Blue Bands on Sleeves, Blue Cap
INT'L. AFFAIR F — B **115**
Dk.b. or br.f.(1983), In Reality—Flitter Flutter
| **15** — **CHARLES WOODS, JR.** (Post Pos. 1)

Watch also for any horse pawing the ground with his front hooves. If you see this, mark "PAW" (pawing) on your program. This horse is telling you that he wants to get the show on the road, (Impatience), a positive signpost for a good race effort.

EXAMPLE:

1 | JOHN FRANKS — WILLIAM I. MOTT
Green, Orange … on White Ball, Orange and White Halves Sleeves, Green Cap
PAW
BOLD SIGNATURE — B **118**
B.c.(1982), Raja Baba—Rock Fever
| **6-5** — **PAT DAY**

By now, all horses should be saddled. Most will enter the walking ring to loosen up and some will not.

I recall one race at Hialeah Park. All horses were saddled and were being led around, except one. This particular horse was faced inward, (most all face outward) and was huddling close to one side. I got a glimpse of his ears and they didn't reveal anything unusual. The horse was perfectly CALM and very still. There was no sign of eagerness whatsoever. The coat wasn't dappled or particularly shiny. He just remained in the stall until led out to be mounted. Naturally, he went wire to wire, paying box car dollars.

A calm horse that can stand still, has been well trained and will start very well from the starting gate. If a calm horse is noted, mark your program with a capital "C."

EXAMPLE:

7 | HUEY McDOWELL AND JOYCE ANGLE — RANDY REED
Green, White "MC," Green Diamonds on White Sleeves
Green Cap
EASTERLY C — B-L **112**
Gr.c.(1982), Explodent—Lady Intrepid
| **10** — **LARRY SNYDER**

Calmness indicates confidence, and is especially positive in the young two year olds.

If you are not already in a good viewing spot at the walking ring, it's time to go find one now.

X.
THE WALKING RING

THE WALKING RING

This is a circle in or close to the paddock area where the horses are loosened up and mounted by the jockeys.

As the horses are being paraded in the walking ring, your next program notations will be regarding the tail of the horse. If the tail is arched, mark a capital "AT" (arched tail). If it isn't, don't mark anything. A tail that is nicely arched and not swishing back and forth is the most positive.

EXAMPLE:

6	WILLIAM B. ROBINSON RICK HILES Red, Green "R," Green Bars on Sleeves Red Cap **RENTED CONDO** AT B **118** B.c.(1982), Delta Oil—Raquel	**4** **EDDIE DELAHOUSSAYE**

When noting the tail, be sure the horse is not preparing to have a bowel movement, for at this time the tail really arches. If the horse is "dumping," note the consistency of his leavings. If light, yellowish-green in color the horse is in good physical condition. If a runny consistency, the horse probably isn't feeling all that well.

Many of my students have asked if a horse "takes a dump," is this a positive? I always answer, "how do you feel after you have?" 90% always answer they feel better. Just because a horse eliminates prior to racing doesn't mean you should run to the window and bet him. You have to have more positive signposts.

If you note the signs of a bad case of worms, even if the horse may be recovering, mark "Worms" on your program. However, the latter is not too often seen at your major race tracks.

Since your eyes are fixed on the tail, glance just below the tail, at the rear of the horse. Between the thighs often you'll see white foam which is called "Kidney Sweat." This foam is caused by the friction of the hind legs and is due to the heat or a slight case of nerves. The sweat is not actually coming from the kidney, but is called kidney sweat because the white foam is often shaped like a kidney. A small amount of kidney sweat is not a negative. Mark your program with a capital "KS," (kidney sweat) only if it's running down the back of the horses leg, or discolored. If the sweat is yellowish-grey, this indicates some kind of infection.

I can recall betting on VANLANDINGHAM two weeks prior to the 1984 Kentucky Derby. I really thought he had a good chance to win. As I watched the post parade on the T.V. monitors, I noticed VANLANDINGHAM had yellow kidney sweat running down the back of his legs. I turned to Jim and said, "VANLANDINGHAM is sick," and tore up my ticket. Naturally, VANLANDINGHAM finished out of the money. I hate myself when I bet on a horse before I get to see it. Thank goodness it wasn't a big bet.

Before leaving "tails," I have two other comments. The #1 most positive arched tail is the "flag tail," where the tail literally comes straight out from the rump, and the long hair drapes down at the end like a flag.

You will see some horses win, when the tail was tight against the buttocks. Always remember—racing is a chess game between trainers and race fans (handicappers).

Some trainers have learned from "show horse" trainers (dressage) a trick of injecting alcohol into the base of the tail. This will immobilize the tail for up to 90 days. (In horse shows, swishing tails lose valuable points).

Total immobility of a tail is unnatural. So if you see a tail that seems "frozen" from paddock to starting gate, this may be the cause.

If the runner is a filly or mare, a patch is often placed over the vaginal opening to prevent air being sucked in during the race. This patch or plug may impede her running action.

Next, glance at the mouth of the horse, see if it has a tongue tie. If it does mark two capital T's on your program, (TT—tongue tie).

EXAMPLE:

3	TIMIR BANERJEE — JENNIE RIGGS Red, Blue "CF," Blue Sleeves Red Cap **GROSHAWKER** TT B-L **112** Ch.c.(1982), Groshawk—Mystery Veil	**30** **MICHAEL McDOWELL**

Often at this time you'll notice white foam around the lips of the horse. This is caused by friction and their constant chewing on the bit. Don't be concerned about the white foam, for many of these horses are winners. If you should see green foam, beware. This horse has been fed recently. Let's face it, I certainly wouldn't race very well after I'd eaten.

Now, glance again at the coat of the horse, record if it is washy, (sweating.) It's after a horse has been saddled that he'll start washing out. If he/she is, record a capital "W" on your program. If not, don't mark anything.

EXAMPLE:

2	CALUMET FARM — MARK CASSE (J. T. Lundy, lessee) Devil's Red, Blue Bars on Sleeves, Red Cap **COLONEL RANIER** W **121** Ch.c.(1982), Riva Ridge—Sweet Tooth	**2** **FRANK LOVATO, JR.**

A washy horse is a nervous horse and will probably not give his best. If a horse is washed out to the point that water drips from his belly, it is an automatic elimination.

There are however, a few horses that do win in a washed out condition. The trick is to keep a record of which ones do. SEATTLE SLEW is a horse that would win washy, and many of his progeny run and win the same way.

What's important here is being able to recognize the difference between the "washy look" and the "wet look." If the horse is wet from being hosed down or a bucket of water thrown over his back, (a cooling off process) you'll be able to see a definite wet/dry line on each side of the horse. If you see a horse that's wet, don't bother to mark your program. This coat is neither positive or negative.

Any sweat should be viewed with common sense judgement. If it is very hot, and you are sweating profusely, then why shouldn't the horse? If it is a light sweat, it will largely evaporate by the time the horse reaches the starting gate.

If the temperature is not extremely hot, washiness is then likely due to nerves. If the horse "settles down," relaxing as the jockey warms him up on the way to the starting gate, the "washy look" will evaporate, and the horse will appear "dry" or "clean."

An important part of your track tools is a good pair of binoculars. If the above occurs, the horse can still be a winner. Other times, you will see the washiness sweat get worse, becoming almost foamy as it runs down the legs and off the stomach. This horse has already "run his race," too much energy has been drained off, and a horse this frightened or angry will also not have his mind on racing.

In keeping these notations on your track program, you can later make lists. You will have lists of horses and the "signposts" that are present and associated with a winning result, and a list of horses that are "down the track" when certain characteristics are seen.

You will more and more automatically remember these. When you have handicapped a horse as a likely winner, and these signs are all present, you can bet with confidence. On the other hand, when you see something that is unexpected, different from what you normally associate with the particular horse, it signals "Beware, why is this happening?"

Now, look for the muscled horse. Train your eyes to glance at the flank of the horse first, then move them towards the rear leg gaskin area, and finally up to the base of the tail.

In the flank area, you're looking for one that is firm and tight, not like jello. On occasion you will see horizontal, washboard type bulges that are formed. If you note a tight flank, make sure it is visible on both sides of the horse. Often you'll see only one or two bulges in this area. Three bulges, however, is more positive. This muscle will be more visible if the horse is prancing. Previously, I have referred to this washboard effect as "Tootsie Rolls," but to eliminate any further harassment of terminology, we will now call it a "Tight Flank," and will record it as a capital "TF" on your program.

EXAMPLE:

6 | A. W. AND D. L. BEST — A. W. BEST
Green, Gold Circled "B"
Green Cap
SHE'S NATIVE TF B-L 115
Ch.f.(1983), Vodika—She's Bad Bad Bad
| 8
DARRELL FOSTER
(Post Pos. 5)

The flank area will also at times appear to be sunken in. This is a sign of weight loss, which is just as negative as being overweight. Fillies, particularly at the age of three, often appear this way. At this age they are maturing sexually and are inclined to leave their feed, especially if overexerted.

If you see a filly filled out (almost fat) in the flank, and not sunken in, mark your program with a capital "FO" (filled out).

EXAMPLE:

10 | MR. AND MRS. EUGENE KLEIN — D. WAYNE LUKAS
Gold, White, Blue and Gold Lightning Bolt, White,
Blue and Gold Lightning Bolt on Sleeves, Gold Cap
Burnished Bright FO B 118
B.f.(1984), Well Decorated—Syntactic by Forward Pass
Bred in Kentucky by Loch Lea Farm
| 7-2
PAT DAY

The fillies will give the appearance of almost looking fat. If she's the only horse in the race, it would be a positive bet. Believe me, they almost always win. I can recall a lone filly that I bet at Meadowlands, during Expo 84, that had the filled out appearance and she paid $62.00. I really like those kind.

As you now glance at the gaskin muscle and up to the base of the tail, you are going to be looking for the "racing muscle." This muscle starts forming near the gaskin area and the farther up towards the base of the tail it goes, the more muscled the horse is. Likewise, if this muscle should branch out into the gaskin muscle, you will note (if a sprint race) this horse will give you a good run for your money. Record a capital "RM" (racing muscle) on your program if the muscle is deep and if it's formed to the base of the tail.

EXAMPLE:

8 | BRUNS M. MEYERS, JR. — ELLIOTT NECAISE
Yellow, Red "M," Red Sleeves
Yellow Cap
LOGAN BURCH RM 114
Ch.c.(1984), Groshawk—Cissy Marjak by Jack Lester
Bred in Mississippi by Bruns M. Meyers, Jr.
| 30
MICKEY SOLOMONE

If you have trouble identifying this muscle, look at the winners of several races. This muscle is extremely visible after the race.

There is another muscle that is called the "conditioning muscle." This muscle forms horizontally along the belly of the horse and measures about two feet in length. This is a positive signpost if visible while the horse is walking. Record on your program a capital "CM" if noticed.

EXAMPLE:

9

JENNY McCALL ANGEL MONTANO

Blue, Gold Halo, Blue Bars on Gold Sleeves

Blue Cap

Jinnys Tap Shoes CM B 114

Ch.c.(1984), Tap Shoes—Athena Mist by Misty Flight

Bred in Kentucky by Walnut Lawn Farm and Avah Ltd.

20

SCOTT MILLER

As the racing muscle, this too is extremely predominant after the race, and will be noticed as the horse breathes and gasps for air.

Any horse that displays a keyed-up attitude by dancing sideways and the shaking of his head, is an anxious horse. He'll be nervous to a certain degree but not unruly like a fractious horse. This may be a positive in some races, but mostly this horse expends his energy before he gets to the starting gate. If spotted, mark your program with a capital "ANX" (Anxious).

EXAMPLE:

6

CAROL STASTNY AND THOMAS E. SHERMAN CLARENCE BREEDLOVE

Cerise, Aqua Blocks, Cerise Cap

J. R.'S PLEASURE ANX B-L 112

Dk.b. or br.g.(1981), Great Vacation—Julie Ruth

6

MICHAEL McDOWELL

By now the jockeys have entered the walking ring. The trainers and owners are usually waiting there to give them last minute instructions and to wish them a safe trip. Try to watch and see if any owner hands or shoves a ticket (presumably winning), in the jockey's boot as he is assisted up into the saddle. Look closely to see how the owners and trainers are dressed. If in suits and ties, one can usually figure they are dressed for a win photograph with their horse after the race.

Once the jockeys have mounted, you normally have one more chance to see each horse pass in front of you. If you happen to be standing in a place where only part of them will pass by, relocate yourself to an area where you'll be able to see them all once again, especially an area where you'll be able to see their rear hooves.

It's time now to watch carefully for what type of shoe the horse is wearing. Remember, watch the rear hooves only. Record the type on your program, where the number of each horse is printed. Record a capital "S" for Stickers, "MC" for Mud caulks, "B" for block heels, and "BS" for a Bar Shoe. If slick-shod, just draw a diagonal line through the horse's program number.

EXAMPLE:

S11 | CELESTINO DILIBERO — GLENN WISMER
Red, White Circled "D" Red Cap
LA MAMA COSA 113
B.f.(1984), Law Maker—House Mother by The Big Boss
Bred in Florida by Celestino Dilibero
STEVE NEFF

12 | ELMER E. MILLER — RONN
Black, Black "EMM" on White Ball, White Black Cap
COAXING CHAD
Dk.b. or br.c.(1984), Linnlear—Angle On Do
Bred in Kentucky by Elmer E. Miller

One day while at the races with a friend of mine, I was doing my paddock recording, and when returning to my seat I would tell her which horses were wearing stickers. If an Exacta race, she would take all the horses wearing them, and box them. There were three Exactas that day, and I believe there was only one race where there were as many as four horses in it that were wearing them. My friend hit all three exacta's—collected $1,200.00—bought me a hamburger. Wasn't that wonderful!!!! Naturally, I sat through all of them not wagering a dime. My fault, of course, but I very rarely bet other than to win or place.

I can't tell you how many times I've bet on what I thought was a positive winner, and was beaten by another horse because he was wearing stickers. Don't get me wrong, I don't want you to go out and bet every horse that's wearing them, for if you do, you'll lose. Each track and day is different. Mark your programs as I've instructed, and watch the first few races to see if any horses with stickers win. If they do, then proceed accordingly, for the track condition probably is deep and horses need that extra traction.

Approximately 75% of all horses racing with stickers on a turf course will be first or second.

Now, I know you are going to ask—"Why don't all the horses wear stickers, if so many are winning with them?" It is costly to switch racing plates (shoes) and many trainer's budgets can not handle the extra expense. There are horses whose hooves are shaped so that an added traction device is not required. Also, a trainer's win intent may not be as valid without them. So be careful, and study what's going on at your track.

By this time the horses are pretty much on the track. Go back to your seat and we'll start watching the post parade.

TIGHT FLANK

Steve Stidham

Look at the muscle on this horse. Notice the washboard effect in the flank area just behind the saddle cloth. This is what I refer to as a "tight flank." (TF) These muscles run horizontally at an angle. Whether you call them "Tootsie rolls," "Havana cigars," or "tight flanks," they are a powerful play when spotted. This horse has a gorgeous shine and a perfect stride. See how the front hooves reach back just to the cinch, and no farther? Betcha can't guess who this is?

TIGHT FLANK

Steve Stidham

Can you spot the "tight flank" on this shot?

FILLED OUT FLANK

Curt Carlson

Notice the flank of this horse. Can you see the "filled out" look? This filly looks almost fat. This is a "filled out" filly. (FO) If you recognize this filly at all, you know she's a winner. LADY'S SECRET.

SUNKEN IN FLANK

Curt Carlson

The flank area of this horse is sunken in. This horse has probably not been eating like he should.

RACING MUSCLE

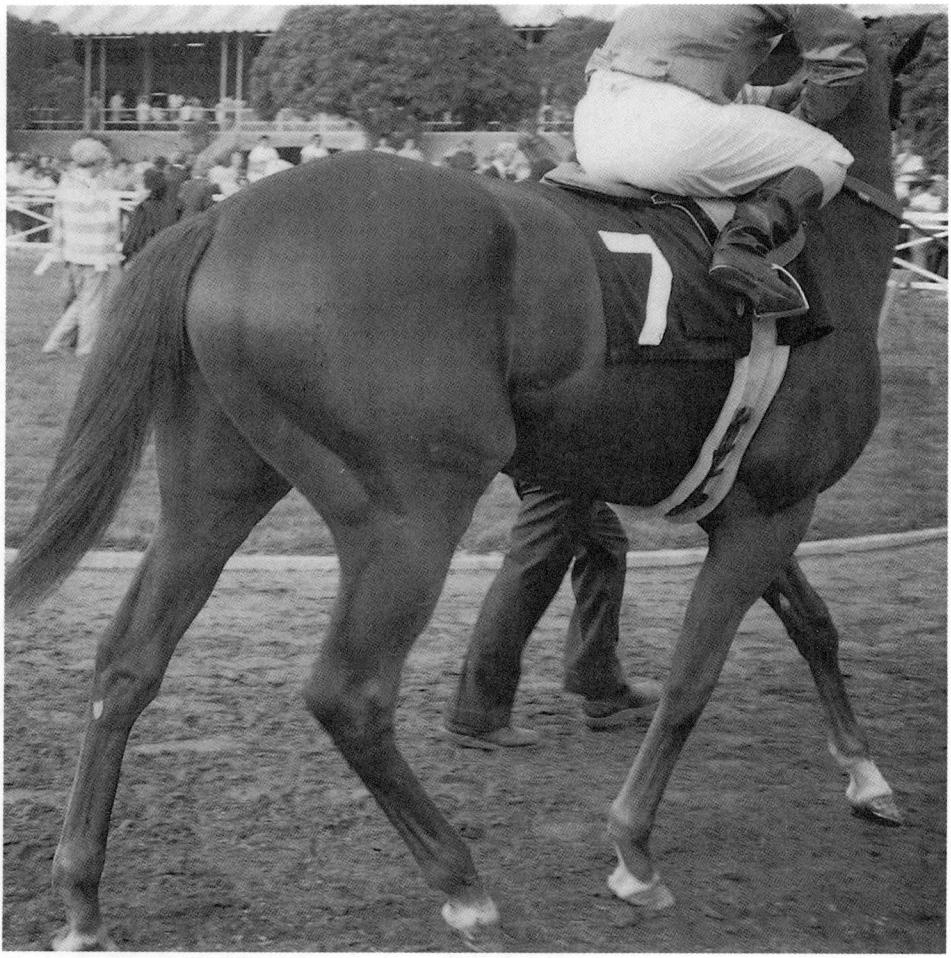

Curt Carlson

Whew! Look at the racing muscle on this horse. (RM) Notice how deep it is and how far up to the base of the tail it goes. The flank area is also tight. The washboard effect is just barely visible.

NO RACING MUSCLE

Curt Carlson

While looking at the exterior extension of this horse you'll find it impossible to locate a visible racing muscle.

MOUTH FOAM

Steve Stidham

Some horses are referred to as having a cold jaw. This horse does not. See the white foam around his mouth. This indicates that he's grabbing the bit and this is a good sign. Some foam will appear also from nervous chewing. I'm a little puzzled about this shot though. See the "Rubber D Bit" he's wearing. Is it because of a sore mouth or because he grabs the bit so hard, and the trainer is trying to protect the horses mouth? I'll go with the latter.

XI.
THE POST PARADE

THE POST PARADE

This is the parade on the track, as horses are walked from the walking ring, past fans in the Turf Club, Club House and Grandstand—to the point that they break into a canter to the Starting Gate.

If the distance of the race is seven furlongs or less, you will have two more chances to see the horse. They will walk past you towards your left, and canter and gallop back to your right, on their way to the starting gate.

At most tracks, if the race distance is more than seven furlongs, and you are not seated right at the finish line, you'll only be able to view the horses one more time.

Often as the horse walks to the left of you, the lead pony will obstruct part of your view. It's disturbing, I know, but it happens supposedly because most lead riders are right handed and they are able to handle their charges better. Truthfully, trainers don't want the public to see "positive signs," and risk the effect on the horse's odds.

There are times when you'll see a horse parade without a lead pony. This may indicate the horse had some problem previously while being paraded and therefore the horse will be more relaxed if parading on his own. Or, the horse may have a tender mouth and may not be able to tolerate any additional jerking on his mouth which occurs when being led.

Sometimes, a horse may not parade at all, but go directly into a gallop off to the starting gate. This may indicate the horse may be a little ouchy or high strung. In either case a quick warm up before the race is all that is needed to either relax the horse or work out the ouchiness.

As the horses move by you the first time, keep in mind their most important concern is to stay on their feet and in balance. A horse that takes quick short steps is either ouchy or is threatened by the surface conditions. A horse with sore knees will produce a wide walk. If any of the above is noted, just draw a line through the horses name on your program. We no longer need be concerned about this horse, for he will not have his mind on racing.

EXAMPLE:

3	W. S. KILROY — NEIL J. HOWARD White, Green Cross Sashes, Green Stripes on Sleeves Green Cap **ROYALTY HILL** **121** B.c.(1984), Naskra—Middle Cornish by Speak John Bred in Kentucky by W. S. Kilroy	**KEITH ALLEN**	**10**

If the distance of the race is over seven furlongs (a route), take particular note of how the rump of the horse is shaped. Normally, the rump is nicely rounded. What you want to see in longer distances is a horse who has a goose rump. This rump looks like it slants diagonally down towards the tail, or more like part of his rump has been chopped off. Many of my distance winners have come from goose rumped horses, especially in claiming races, and those that are carrying light weight. If you note a goose rumped horse, mark a capital "GR" on your program, only if the distance is a route, and the longer the better.

EXAMPLE:

7
BILL MOOK, ROBERT SNELL AND WILLIAM THIMGAN — BILL MOOK
Aqua, Orange Horse, Orange Sleeves, Aqua Cap
Mr. Zippity Do Dah B **121**
Ch.c.(1984), Exuberant—Catchy Little Tune by Daryl's Joy
Bred in Florida by Robert Snell
3
JULIO ESPINOZA

Have you noticed any horse shoving his nose into the neck of the lead pony yet? If so, just write "BET" across the horses name. This is a definite positive and should be considered a major contender.

EXAMPLE:

6
CLAIBORNE FARM (Mrs. A. B. Hancock, Jr.) — STEVE PENROD
Orange, Orange Cap
ADMIT A... B **114**
Ch.c.(1984), Believe It—Alyne Que by Raise A Native
Bred in Kentucky by Claiborne Farm
15
EDDIE DELAHOUSSAYE

Often you'll see a horse with his head over the neck of the lead pony, walking sideways. This is a nervous, frightened response, and a negative.

Have you seen any horse move his head up and down, as to indicate, Yes, Yes, Yes, I'm ready to race? This is a positive signpost, so mark your program with capitals "YYY."

EXAMPLE:

5
RED PORT PARTNERS (Leslie R. Millman, et al) — LARRY MAYO
Green, White Braces, Green Cap
TEMPLAR HILL B **114**
B.c.(1984), Temperence Hill—Sobriquet by Lt. Stevens
Bred in Kentucky by Lillie F. Webb
20
JOE IMPARATO

As the horses are turned around on the track to head back, they first will canter and often times break into a gallop. Again, watching the rear hooves, look for those that bring their hooves onto the surface at just about the same time, just digging in. To clarify this a little better, the rear hooves will be reaching the surface somewhat like a rabbit. The Thoroughbred, however, is incapable of doing it exactly like a rabbit, but the closer together, the more strength the horse will have. This is a definite positive, especially if noted on an off track. If this is noted, mark your program with a capital "RC" (rear close).

EXAMPLE:

4	JACK MONDEL — RONALD L. BENSHOFF White, Silver Panels, Silver Bars on Sleeves White Cap **TOUGH IT OUT** B **121** Ch.c.(1984), Encino—Nanny Jeanne by Encinto Bred in New Jersey by Jack Mondel	**DON BRUMFIELD**	**8**

For your last look at all the horses, try to distinguish which is the biggest horse and which is the smallest. If big, mark your program with a capital "BH," (big horse) if small, mark a capital "SH" (small horse).

EXAMPLE:

5	FARID SEFA — WILLIAM I. MOTT Gold, Red Diamonds, Gold "S" on Red Diamond on Sleeves, Gold Cap **HABITONIA** B-L **118** B.h.(1980), Habitony—Latonia Thrush	**PAT DAY**	**7-5**

This is my Clydesdale versus the Shetland Pony theory. If the track condition is deep you will find the Shetland Pony (small horse) in the winner's circle. The small horse naturally will skim across the surface. The big horse however, if not competing with a small horse, will be in the winner's circle, for he will have the stamina to win.

The Clydesdale, (big horse) on a fast flat track, especially in a route, will have the strength for the distance and will usually be in the money. The Shetland pony, however, if not competing with a big horse, will breeze nicely again to the winner's circle.

The "Shetland pony" will generally measure 15 hands or less, and will appear "tiny" in the post parade, when compared to the other horses. The lighter weight, and commonly smaller feet, cause the horse to literally run on top of the track surface. Their hooves are not punching as deeply into the heavier and tacky "bottom" of the track, and much less energy is being used in each stride. From Kentucky Derby winner LITTLE CURRENT to currently racing HERAT, the first to recognize this "edge" collects the longshot prices.

The "Clydesdale" will approach 17 hands or more, the saddle and rump of the horse will look like it is six inches higher than the other horses. Many of your classic "champions" fall into this category.

O.K., we've seen all we could. The horses have passed by and are now on their way to the starting gate.

Binoculars will let you watch what goes on at the starting gate. Even in the Breeder's Cup races, you may see a horse plant his/her feet firmly, legs braced, refusing to enter the starting gate. The horse may ultimately be forced in, literally carried if necessary by a half dozen members of the gate crew. Note what happens on your program. The horse is either hurting, unschooled, or traumatized by something that has happened. You would not want to bet this horse again unless later races prove this has been corrected.

The starting gate is where you will see at some tracks some of the bad aspects of racing—a trainer sneaking a tongue-tie on at the last minute (no equipment can be legally added after the horse has left the paddock), a gate handler holding the tail of the favorite, so that the horse breaks dead last by many lengths.

There are also "racing luck" things that happen there. Sometimes a horse rears and goes over backwards, naturally tossing the jockey in the process. When this happens, the horse really should be scratched, but at many tracks the horse will be put back into the starting gate.

Do you think either the horse or the jockey will have much interest in running a competitive race? Not likely. Also, a Thoroughbred is one of the most fragile beings. Often, a horse will be seen to stumble when coming out of the starting gate. Sometimes the horse will literally go to his knees before getting himself together and trying to catch up.

I will not bet on any horse that "flips" in the starting gate, or stumbles out of the gate, or falls in a race in any future race until there are totally positive signs that the horse is all right. These bad luck happenings are where many injuries occur, and many such horses never win again.

We have all these markings on our program, and have just a few minutes to put it all together before we make our wager. Let's get started.

GOOSE RUMP

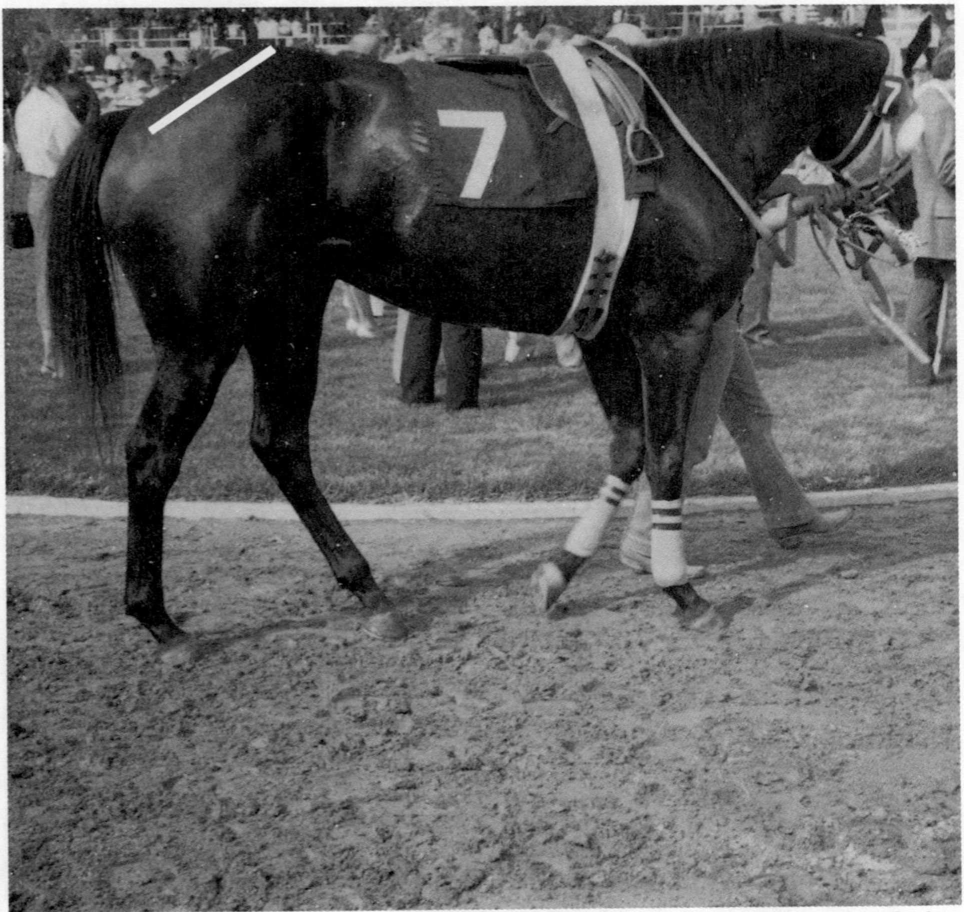

Curt Carlson

This shot is a good example of a "goose rump." (GR) Notice how chopped off the rump appears. I've drawn a white line across the rump so it will show the chopped off look more clearly. This particular horse I would not wager on due to the other body signs he is displaying. He has that "sunken in" flank appearance, plus if you look close you'll be able to see some white foam in the flank area which means he's starting to wash-out.

NO GOOSE RUMP

Curt Carlson

The rump of this horse is normal. I've outlined the area in white so you can compare it with the previous "goose rump" photo. This horse also has a "conditioning muscle." I've outlined it in white also. See how it runs lengthwise across the horse's belly. The flank area of this horse is nicely filled out and I see a nice shine. I might wager on one like this if there's nothing better. However, this shot was from the Breeder's Cup so I'm sure we would have found something.

GRASS STRIDE

Steve Stidham

This is one high stepper. Look at how high he gets his left front hoof off the ground. That looks like about twenty-four inches off the surface instead of twelve. Look how straight he's extending that foreleg. This one needs to get off the dirt and onto the grass.

DIRT STRIDE

Steve Stidham

This horse has a good dirt stride. His right front hoof is only about six inches off the ground. Please note the length of this horses stride—beautifully straight and almost extended beyond his nose.

GRASS vs. DIRT

Unknown

This is a fairly good comparison shot of a dirt stride and a grass stride. The horse in the lead has a grass stride and the other one has a dirt stride.

XII.
PUTTING IT ALL TOGETHER

PUTTING IT ALL TOGETHER

The more positive signposts recorded on any one horse the better. Let's first refresh our memory of all the positive signpost abbreviations.

AT — Arched Tail
BH — Big Horse (Clydesdale)
BL — Bute and Lasix
CM — Conditioning Muscle
DAP — Dappled Coat
FO — Filled Out Filly
GR — Goose Rump (routes only)
L — Lasix (1st or 2nd time)
MC — Mud Caulks
NS — Nice Shiny Coat
PAW — Pawing The Ground
RM — Racing Muscle
RC — Rear Hooves Close
S — Stickers
SH — Small Horse
T — On Toes (prancing)
TF — Tight Flank
TT — Tongue Tie
YYY — Yes, Yes, Yes

So we know the positives, now let's take the more common ones viewed and separate them into different distances.

FOR SPRINTS (seven furlongs or less)

BH — Big Horse
TF — Tight Flank
AT — Arched Tail
DAP — Dappled Coat
T — On Toes (prancing)
NS — Nice Shiny Coat

RM — Racing Muscle
TT — Tongue Tie
S — Stickers
L — Lasix (1st or 2nd time)

FOR ROUTES (seven furlongs or more)

GR — Goose Rump
TF — Tight Flank
T — On Toes (prancing)
RM — Racing Muscle
RC — Rear Hooves Close
BH or SH—Big or Small Horse
TT — Tongue Tie
NS — Nice Shiny Coat
DAP— Dappled Coat

SAMPLE RACES

We've reviewed all the positives signposts, now let's look at what we've recorded for the horses on the first race of the day.

All sample race track conditions are labeled fast.

FIRST RACE

6 1/2 Furlongs — 3 Year Olds — Claiming $12,500

1	TT	RM	ANX	T	RC	120
2	TT	RM	KS			118
3	DAP	AT				120
4	BH	TF	AT			111
5s						116
6	TF	AT				118
7	TF	T				118
8	AT	RC				115

The #1 horse had a tongue-tie, displayed a racing muscle, was a little anxious, prancing on his toes and looked as though his rear hooves were hitting the ground about the same time. Five positives—it looks like we should place our bet on this one, but carrying 120 pounds worries us a little, especially on the first race of the day. Let's look further at what we've got.

The #2 horse is a no bet situation for we noted kidney sweat and wouldn't have marked it, unless it was discolored or running down his leg.

The #3 horse looked healthy and displayed pride, but there again he has to carry 120 pounds.

The #4 horse seemed to be the Clydesdale of the field, had a nice tight flank and a beautiful arched tail. Oh yes, note he's only carrying 111 pounds, and is second in the number of positives we've recorded.

The #5 horse is the only horse wearing stickers in the race and didn't show any other positive signposts, so we'll pass on him.

The #6 horse has tight flanks and an arched tail.

The #7 horse also displayed tight flanks and was prancing nicely.

The #8 horse had an arched tail, rear hooves were close and he is only carrying 115 pounds.

Also note, none of the horses are medicated.

O.K., we've eliminated the #2 and #5. We should also eliminate the high weighted horses, because it's the 1st race of the day, and the track is probably deep. That leaves us with the #4, 6, 7, & 8. Which one would you bet on, and why? If you chose #4, YOU'RE A WINNER. He had the most positive signposts recorded and he was the biggest horse in the race carrying the lightest weight. The #6 horse was second and the #7 horse was third. Note, all three horses displayed a tight flank. Yes, this was an actual race and the payoffs were:

#4	$10.40	$6.60	$6.00
#6		$7.20	$6.00
#7			$7.80

You did well. The next race you are on your own. YOU PICK THE WINNER.

SECOND RACE

6 1/2 FURLONGS	3 Year Old Fillies			Claiming $16,000
1	DAP			112
2	RC	T	AT	107
3	DAP			118
4s	TT	RM	(too thin)	107
5				112
6s	DAP			115
7s	BH			112
8	AT			118

NOTE: On the #4 horse, I could see ribs on the horse in front of the saddle cloth, so I marked "too thin" on my program. Noticeable ribs behind the saddle cloth is O.K., but in front is a negative.

Race results will be printed after WATCHING THE RACES.

Now for the next race—Let's try a route. The circled numbers below indicate the age of the horse.

THIRD RACE

1 1/16 Miles		Fillies & Mares 4 Years Old & Up	Claiming $10,000
1	⑤	DAP	107
2s	④	T GR	107
3	⑤	BH W	112
4	④	DAP NS	112
5	⑥	W	112
6	⑤	GR	115
7	④	TT	112
8	⑤	RM BH DAP TT RC	107
9s	⑦	TF	109

In this race, if you don't pick the winner, you'd better re-read my instructions. In fact, you should be able to pick the trifecta in this race. Results printed after WATCHING THE RACES.

Let's try just one more.

FOURTH RACE

1 1/16 Miles		4 Years Old & Up	Claiming $12,500
1	⑥	(WET) TT	109
2	④	YYY	120
3	④	GR W T	114
4	④		114
5	④		114
6	④	AT	114
7	④	AT	114
8	④	RM AT T	114
9	⑧	TT RM AT	109

NOTE: The #1 horse has "WET" recorded. This is not the washy horse, but the one that was cooled off with a bucket of water.

This race, too, should be fairly simple for you to pick the winner. Yes, race results are printed after WATCHING THE RACES.

XIII.
WATCHING THE RACES

WATCHING THE RACES

It's now time to watch the race and your best viewing is in front of a T.V. monitor.

What you see during each race is as important to record as the positive signposts are, for each day's program will be your key to winning future races. At the end of each race day, I tear the cover off the program so the date is visible and file them in date order.

When I need to check on a horse that's racing again, I check my programs and transfer any trouble notations and/or positive signposts that were recorded previously, to the *Daily Racing Form.* What's important is to know when a positive change occurs and the only way to do that is by keeping records.

O.K., back to watching the races. Note any horse that stumbles or has a slow start. This would be a negative racing back. Record any horse that races extremely wide. This could indicate ouchiness or the need of a stronger jockey. Take particular note of any horse that's blocked or forced to check. This could be an excellent playback, if after being blocked, a good race effort developed.

The most advantageous noting to make is regarding the stride of the horse. Their stride can actually be measured and can be determined by the slant of the shoulder. The straighter the shoulder the shorter the stride.

A horse who curls his front hooves back just slightly past the cinch and then extends them out straight about 6 inches off the dirt, would have a good DIRT STRIDE. If the horse extends his hooves out 10 to 12 inches off the dirt, this would be a good GRASS STRIDE.

I have had several wins playing back horses on the turf that raced on the dirt, with grass strides. Many of them paid excellent prices.

A horse who brings his front hooves back almost to the flank area is breaking over at the knees. This horse will take a fraction of a second longer to get his hooves extended forward, and when you add those fractions up, they all count. A horse that does this is using more energy and will likely tire quicker.

Another thing to watch closely for is any horse that is pulled up quickly after crossing the finish line. This indicates a serious problem and I hesitate to wager on any problem horse until he proves himself. Pulling a horse up quickly is the easiest way of injuring his ankles and tendons. Most jockeys are aware of this and will not do it unless there is a problem. I record on my program SHORT BACK, when this occurs.

There are so many things to watch for and so much concentration is required in order to truly gain from all your hard work and effort. It's ALMOST impossible for one individual to keep track of everything, but believe me it gets easier the more you practice.

If you're a serious horse player, the worst thing to do is take an inexperienced horse player to the track with you and try to make decisions and wager. That's impossible. Go by yourself or take someone that's as knowledgeable as you are and work together on the signposts. Teamwork is always easier.

Good Luck to you and I hope we'll meet at the same cashier's window someday.

Now for the race results:

SECOND RACE

#2	$18.40	$6.40	$3.60
#7		$3.60	$2.60
#5			$3.00

The #2 horse had the most positives recorded and again was carrying light weight. I love the lighter weighted horses, especially in routes and in claiming races. The #7 horse, who placed, could have tired a little due to the stickers he was wearing. He was a big horse and the track was still pretty deep. Did you pick the winner? I hope so.

THIRD RACE

#8	$15.00	$7.60	$4.00
#2		$14.20	$8.00
#6			$8.60

Did you get this one? Again the #8 horse had the most positives recorded and was the Clydesdale of the race. The place and show horses were the only ones that had the goose rump. Remember the goose rump in routes? Nice payoffs huh?

FOURTH RACE

#9	$5.80	$3.00	$2.80
#1		$3.40	$3.00
#3			$6.60

This one should have been easy also. The two oldest and light weighted horses came in one, two, and the show horse had a goose rump.

XIV.
THE BUSINESS OF RACING

THE BUSINESS OF RACING!
By My Better Half

In earlier chapters, there were references to drugs and "buzzers." Those who handicap Thoroughbred races would be wrong to ignore the existence of either. They would also be wrong to over-react.

Once you know the signs, you will know when one or the other is involved in a race outcome (granted that rarely will you get your money back after you have seen your horse beaten by a buzzer in the stretch). If the signs aren't there, something else caused the loss. Most losing tickets are the product of handicapping judgement errors, or often "racing luck."

Let's look at a race tracker's worst nightmare—a Racing Secretary that is a Superman at writing race conditions; all horses on the backside are well-bred and in perfect shape; all trainers are equal in competence at all distances and class levels; and each jockey is as good as every other. The nightmare ending—nine races per day with 8–12 noses side-by-side at the wire.

This would be a horrifying dream even to owners, inferring that every race was the product of "racing luck," determined by which horse's nose is straight out, maximally extended in the win photo. (And consider the inference to Exactas and the Pick Six).

But this won't happen; it IS only a nightmare. The horse player must prepare himself/herself for the real world, as it exists today, and as we can project it toward the future.

The horse player/handicapper has a right to expect competent officiating, an absence of buzzers and unlawful drugs, and access to areas of information which are a reasonable expectation of the consumer.

All this is coming, and possibly soon. When the economics of racing intersect with a sagging national economy, we can look forward to some specific changes: (1) a national Rules of Racing; (2) Thoroughbred racing henceforth defined in law as an industry in interstate commerce; (3) a national OTB; and (4) application of technology that will allow a race fan to watch all aspects of a racing day on a cable channel, pausing at will to telephone a bet into the track parimutuel system.

This is NOT science fiction; all hardware and technology needed exists today (like the TV picture tube, waiting for its "time"). It is a literal certainty for sometime in the 1990's.

While race fans will benefit via improved racing, it WILL NOT change some of the basic facts of life. It will still be lawful for trainers and jockeys to wager (as long as not against themselves). In the process, it will not be in their interests to telegraph intentions to the crowd. Trainers will always need parimutuel profits as an added cash flow; and this will remain a legitimate goal.

Ironically, when the "outlaw minority," relying on illegal "edges" to reach the winner's circle, are deprived of their contraband, we will see more races won by trainer brain power; each trainer will be a handicapping adversary. A reasonable fan cannot fault anything within the Rules of Racing at that point, so even more the wins will go to those who do their homework (there will never be a "free lunch").

A racing stable with parimutuel goals seeks the highest possible ratio of win percentage vs average payoff. It will always be so. A profit-motivated race fan will succeed only if setting and meeting the same goal. CHALK KILLS!

As we enter the age of racing "high tech," the sitting-at-home Player may have the best of it in many ways. He/she will have a better viewing advantage for a longer time than those craning necks to see around corners at the track. The refrigerator means less time lost to standing in line for a beer or hot dog, allowing closer monitoring of the Tote Board (always in the upper, right hand corner of the screen).

When at the track, the individual naturally tends to focus on the horse in which there is a betting interest. In addition, there is so much to do between races that few have time to watch race re-runs (and, even when possible, one fights the crowd for a viewing opportunity).

This marriage of racing and technology can go beyond the present Nevada Race Book offerings, where even now we see two re-runs, and usually the head-on stretch drive previously reserved to officials on high. Added to this is 5–10 minutes of walking ring and paddock footage (at the track unavailable to any not prepared for a long walk—and stairs—every half hour), and roughly double the post parade footage—as enhanced by the ZOOM lens.

As simulcasting expands to Cable-TV, one can expect this much coverage, and inevitable other goodies that can be relayed electronically. And, of course, the home player would connect up a handy, dandy VCR, allowing infinite later re-runs—collecting "PLAY BACKS" and "HORSES TO WATCH" from "trip handicapping" analysis.

Oh yes, another thing you can count on in the 1990's—while gradually tracks are converted to the synthetic surface introduced at Remington Park, and we will be rid of the damnable sand that can whimsically create track biases that blow away the previous night's work—it will also be bankable that too many horses will run in too many races at too many race tracks each calendar year.

There are two scenarios. Smart trainers will protect their horses. Their shots at the winner's circle will be folded in amongst 30–40 races per year where entry is to help the Racing Secretary fill races. In the process, individual Thoroughbred "Class" and "Form" will be colored by these exercise races.

Trainers that are not-so-smart will push each horse in every race (a naiveté of the present Rules of Racing). Those that haven't broken down by late summer will be candidates to tucker out and go off form, literally one race to the next. In the last half of the calendar year, the horse player can anticipate the lowest percentage of winning favorites. The majority of races will be won by horses that seem off-the-wall to Speed/Pace devotees and to any and all that don't understand the business of racing vs the Thoroughbred as a professional athlete.

The winning horse player, now into the 21st Century, will have put together three specialties: (1) Trainer data that will separate the smart from the unsmart. This will emerge from trip handicapping time investment and notations; (2) a command of post parade and paddock analysis (those "winning effort" days, as they occur per trainer and horse, will be "tipped" by equipment and Thoroughbred signposts); and (3) an optimum money management approach to race betting as an investment.

XV.
RACE BOOKS

A LAS VEGAS RACE BOOK TOUR WITH JIM

At some time, a reader might be tempted to apply total handicapping skills to Nevada Race Books. A Las Vegas vacation? Not everyone is hooked on the slots. Many in the U.S., however, are not aware of exactly how Race Books operate. How does one approach this area of competition?

Even to those residing in Las Vegas, it is awesome to watch the explosion in numbers of Race and Sports Books over the last three years. The annual gross of R/S Books to the Casinos is now passing the slots, previously the #1 bread-and-butter cash flow.

Simulcasting begins with a contractual relationship between the race track and a disseminator licensed by the Nevada Gaming Commission. The disseminator charges to the Race Books a daily fee that correlates to gross (the more business you do, the more you pay).

Tracks simulcasting to Nevada include: Aqueduct, Belmont, Saratoga, Santa Anita, Hollywood Park, Del Mar, Bay Meadows, Golden Gate, Hawthorne Park, Garden State, Meadowlands, Monmouth Park, and the harness track meets of New Jersey. These are the staples, and will be carried by most Race Books.

Disseminators also bring in the signals of Pimlico, Laurel, Gulfstream, Hialeah, Calder, Philadelphia Park, and such random options as Los Alamitos harness racing, Bay Meadows harness racing, Tucson dog racing, and some of the "California Fair Track circuit." More recently, simulcasted tracks have included Longacres, Balmoral, and three Florida dog tracks. So the time has come when ANY track may appear in Nevada.

The individual Race Book offerings vary. Generally, management is going to take enough signals to create at least 12 hours of action. They will select at least two signals where, because of time differences, races begin 9:30–10:30 AM, Las Vegas time. They may then add the Chicago track, a noon starter when open, following with the California tracks that begin in the early afternoon. New Jersey Thoroughbred and harness tracks start at 5:00 PM (plus Bay meadows on Fridays). Those using West Coast harness racing and/or "the dogs" will have 7 PM starts, last action finishing about 11 PM. (These few Race Books create 14 hours of non-stop ACTION).

The Race Book, itself, will have five or six tracks "On Board," which means they will be represented by huge, vertical wall boards, a section 10–15 feet high for each race on that track's card for the day. These in most Race Books will be sheets of paper that list the post positions, vertically, by a "house (code) number." (EX: the first race of Aqueduct will be #1–20, the second race #21–39, etc.—Hollywood Park's first race will be 701–720, second race 721–740).

The code numbers are assigned to every horse entered, as they appear in the *Daily Racing Form* "past performance" listings. When betting, the player MUST use this assigned number. At New York tracks, it is not uncommon to have 6–10 "also eligibles;" #49, the ninth also-eligible may scratch into the race, and win up in the #8 post position. But in betting and collecting, you would have to have a ticket on #49.

In the morning, these sheets will commonly reflect all the races at Aqueduct/Belmont, Hawthorne (if running), the Race Book's preference as to Florida, Maryland, and Pennsylvania—one or two of same, and the open tracks for the Los Angeles and San Francisco racing circuits. About 3 PM, as racing is completed at the Eastern tracks, the wall boards are pulled down, and sheets are put up for the evening tracks.

Race Books also carry tracks "off the board." These are not represented by wall boards. Usually, these will be tracks with less information available, and the types and amount of betting will be further restricted. "Off the Board" wagering will hinge to top tier tracks, that either are not simulcasted, or where the Race Book has not contracted for the signal. But they will also include additional tracks such as Oaklawn, Keenland, Churchill Downs, and California Fair Meet tracks that are never simulcasted.

Each Race Book makes up its selections of track offerings based on individual preferences (and sometimes prejudices). And there are tracks they will NEVER take—definitely out of prejudice viewed as "trainer game" tracks. In truth, while these negative perceptions have a long history, today they could extend to many that ARE carried and available to the bettor.

The first decision a horse player must make (and as per knowledge necessary) is "do you want to do some handicapping the night before?" Most Race Books are operated by Las Vegas "Strip" hotel/casinos. They will provide the *Daily Racing Form* FREE, or if there is a charge, they will refund it at the end of the day, but most WILL NOT make it available (neither Eastern nor Western edition) until 8:30 AM on race day.

If wishing a head start in handicapping (absolutely necessary if tackling multiple tracks), one must learn how to "beat the system." The Eastern and Western editions of the *Daily Racing Form* usually arrive here by 7 PM, and delivery is then made by a local news service. Based on their routing, the forms are usually at the Palace Station (Sahara West & Rancho Drive) before the Race Book closes.

The Gold Coast, one of the newest casino/hotels (and which we frequent), is located at the juncture of Freeway I-15 and Flamingo Road. The next day's

Racing Forms are available at the race book until it closes, and via the Sports Book cashier's window until it closes (which is "never" during football season, 11 PM the rest of the year).

Jerry's Nugget (Las Vegas Boulevard at Lake Mead Boulevard in North Las Vegas) does not run evening races, but they will sell the *Daily Racing Form* out of the main cashier's cage (usually by 10 PM and after).

Anyone West Coast oriented will find the Western edition in the gift shops of Little Caesar's, Barbary Coast, Stardust, and Palace Station after the Race Books close (usually after 11 PM). BUT, for these you'll have to pay the regular price and no rebate. The Race Book reimbursements hinge only to papers that carry their individual "stamp." Also, sometimes a Race Book manager may not like the idea of gift shop competition, and suddenly the DRF disappears from same. So these availabilities can be subject to change.

Presuming the *Daily Racing Form* was obtained the night before, the player has a chance to choose from up to 70 individual races. It's a "field day" for the "specialist." Whether one targets on Stakes and Allowance races only, two-year-old competitions, claimers, or "gimmick races" for action—there are many of each to choose from, as many as can be reasonably handled.

The next objective is 8:30 AM arrival at the Race Book of your choice. Between 8:30 and 9:30 AM, the disseminator will broadcast scratches, jockey changes, weather conditions, and for some tracks, Lasix information. Various Race Books have prime spots for TV viewing, and the later the arrival, the poorer the viewing perspective of the simulcasts.

Preferences in Race Books hinge, naturally, to personal opinion. Three—Caesar's Palace, Las Vegas Hilton and Circus Circus—do not use the conventional "wall boards." This information is in computer-programmed lighting (red). Readability is difficult for anyone wearing glasses unless seated dead center, and even then the tracks on the left or right side of the room will be blurred. This is the price one must pay for "elegance" and "high tech."

These also have huge TV screens, but the larger the screen, the dimmer and more blurred the picture. Use of paddock and post parade scrutiny is all but impossible, where TV sets do not render a sharp image.

The Gold Coast is a good example of a Race Book with an optimum number of T.V. monitors, well-placed. If anything, the customer on first experience will be a bit "overwhelmed;" there is so much to see. The biggest challenges immediately become concentration and organization. (The "off-the-board" tracks and "on-board" tracks without simulcasting, require closing of betting approximately five minutes before the horses are in the gate. A Race Book staff member will post on the wall board sheet a "post time," and you work from there. It is very easy to have a bet planned for Track "A," get immersed in the post parade at Track "B," only to find it's too late that the Track "A" race has been "closed" and you are "shut out."

Selecting the Race Book for optimum viewing also requires some seasonal considerations. Caesars Palace, Bally's, and others are "forget it" if there is a big convention in town. These and others can be mad houses during

Fall football, as Sports Books and Race Books are usually side-by-side. The decibel level from Sports Book screamers is unreal, not to mention those who will take up Race Book seats and crane their neck to see Sports Book TV monitors.

A little inside information is warranted as to the Barbary Coast. Their basic Race Book is very nice, but hard to find. Walk from the Sports Book (inside the Casino) toward the Strip entrance. After you have passed the main Cashier's Counter and restrooms, you will come to a long bar. The Race Book is behind the bar, complete with tables and chairs, a half dozen TV screens (good images), and its own sellers and cashiers (and wall boards).

There are so many permutations of Race Book layouts, advantages and disadvantages, that the visitor should probably start his/her campaign on Tuesday, the closest to "dark" day (only a few tracks running, nationally), and use the day for a "cook's tour." This would perhaps start with Sam's Town, at Flamingo and Boulder Highway (coming from Boulder Dam). Continuing North on Boulder Highway, visit the Showboat, and then get back on Boulder Highway and continue North.

Just beyond the Showboat, the road takes an angled left and becomes Fremont Street, which leads to and becomes the center of downtown Las Vegas. Here you can check out Union Plaza (the largest downtown), the Freemont, El Cortez, even slum at "Leroy's."

Backtracking east a few blocks will put one at Las Vegas Boulevard. Before hitting "The Strip," take a left north-bound for about a mile to Jerry's Nugget, then reverse and head Southbound on Las Vegas Boulevard. At this point, you will also have seen 90% of the area's pawn shops (hopefully, these will never be needed).

The first Race Book in this Southbound tour of "The Strip" will be the smallest Race Book in Nevada, a literal "closet" in the casino part of Vegas World. There is no seating area, wall boards, or other amenities, but allegedly owner Bob Stupak will take bets (size) that make other establishments shudder.

The "Strip" really starts at Sahara Avenue. Progressing South, the Sahara, Sands, and Riviera, will be on the left, the Stardust (one of the largest), Circus Circus, and Frontier (one of the newest) on your right. You will then be at Spring Mountain Road. From this intersection, opposite the Fashion Mall, everything South until you reach Caesars Palace, will be Steve Wynn's new Mirage. On the left heading South, will be the Holiday Inn and Barbary Coast.

From present appearances, the strip hotel/casinos that do not have Race & Sports books are planning on adding same. North of Tropicana, three new and huge complexes have been announced, and a fourth across from the Gold Coast. All four (scheduled for 1990 opening) promise "the biggest and best."

Until Wynn's mammoth project is complete, the others to consider are the Palace Station and the two new kids on the block, the Las Vegas Hilton and the Gold Coast. The Las Vegas Hilton is on Paradise Road, which runs parallel to the Strip on the East, next to the Convention Center. On the East side of the existent Casino and Hotel, the Hilton has created a new building to house the Race and Sports books, with its own parking facilities. Loop around behind the Convention Center and hotel, and you will find it easily.

For the Gold Coast, head West on Flamingo from the intersection of Flamingo Road and Las Vegas Boulevard. (This is at present the "action corner" of the strip, the intersection corners occupied by Barbary Coast, Bally's, formerly MGM Grand, the Dunes, and Caesars Palace). Heading West on Flamingo, I-15 is immediately behind Caesars—take the overpass, once over the freeway, there will be two stoplights (Highland and Valley View), and The Gold Coast will rise above you on the right, just past the second stop light (Valley View).

Leaving here, turn on to Valley View, heading North. You will pass within a few blocks of the Selvidge residence as you approach Sahara Avenue. Turn right on to Sahara, heading East, and at Rancho Drive—just before the I-15 freeway, Palace Station will loom on the right. This tour can be completed in an afternoon of cruising (if going first class, allocate $15 for valet parking, a buck per stop). (When downtown, would recommend the parking garage of the Las Vegas Club. Everything else is within walking distance. The Las Vegas Club is one of our favorite Sports Books, and the cashier will validate your parking card).

As you make this tour in search of the Race Book that most suits your personal preference, you should make notes at each as to what they offer as betting propositions.

All Race Books have a house Quinella on every race (payoff is half of the track price to Place times the track payoff on the Win). Increasingly, we find the Quinella more productive than Exactas. On Exactas, they pay what the track pays—to a $202 maximum (per $2 of wagering). Exactas are being hammered so hard at many tracks—when the exacta on a $2 bet pays $28, presumably the player took the horses both ways, $4 invested, $24 profit. On the same race, the Quinella formula might pay $24 on a $2 bet. So a $4 quinella outlay brings a $20 increase in net profits.

Some books will pay to a $303 maximum per $2 bet, whether it is an Exacta, Daily Double, or Win Bet. Some Race Books will offer Trifecta betting on the last races at New York and New Jersey tracks; the Union Plaza offers its own "Pick Six" (up to $500,000 maximum payoff). Several—like Palace Station—offer a "Twin Q." There are a variety of other enticements. One at present gives you a free breakfast if you bet $10 on any race. Others give a free Daily Double ticket to "early birds."

Somewhere on the wall near either seller's or cashier's windows EVERY Race Book has a big Board that lists its "House Rules." A serious horse player should copy these down for each establishment. If not visible, on request they will clarify any other variables, such as how they treat DRF dissemination, inducements (including drink and food comps,) betting advantages (as relates to competitors). There are varying permutations of straight parlays and round robin parlays. In some spots with new computers, you can bet a 5-race round robin (combining different tracks, if you wish) on a single ticket.

Not knowing the Rules (and differences) can be costly. As but one example, in Exactas and Trifectas, an entry covers all the bases. if you like 1B (as per ESTRAPADE in the Arlington Million), you also get 1A and 1C in your Exacta or Trifecta. So a "box" of 1B with #2, #3, and #7 gives you actually every combination of six horses. Better yet, suppose #2 is also an entry (very common in New York and Los Angeles). Boxing four horses might give you all permutations of up to eight starters. NOT SO in the Quinella at most establishments. If the order of finish is 2B-1C-1B-5, you don't get paid off, as an Exacta or Trifecta would do, on 2–1–5. To collect the Quinella, you would have to have a ticket on 2B with 1C, specifically.

Once you have selected the one or more Race Books that suit your needs, it is then time to combine the pre-race handicapping judgements, off *Daily Racing Form* evaluation, with what can be gleaned from visual appraisal from the simulcast coverage. (So Jim will sign off, and Trillis will continue).

As we continue, you will note Jim's writing is much more complex then mine. O.K., let's get on with it.

Initially, the race viewing at the Palace Station and Jerry's Nugget were the best by our standards. We now prefer the Gold Coast. Believe me, neither of us are getting paid to plug any of the casinos, but we have been to nearly all of the race books in town and find the atmosphere, viewing, friendliness, and accuracy—all can be found at the latter.

When entering the race book of your choice, first locate a good seat close to a T.V. monitor. If the race book has their screens elevated, do not sit too close, for you'll end up with a stiff neck by the end of the day. I would suggest arriving at least 45 minutes before the track or tracks you've chosen to play start racing. This will give you enough time to get a good seat, a cup of coffee, and time to locate the individual entry sheets.

The entry sheets for each track are provided to the public at no charge and are located in bins at one end of the teller windows. They are 11 x 14 sheets or longer, white in color, and are identical to what's printed on the wallboard, or displayed in colored lights. Each entry sheet will include the name of the track, track surface condition, code (betting) number, and name of the horse, jockey, morning line odds, and the weight the horse will carry. If there are any scratches, they will be crossed off with a straight line drawn through the horse's name. Once you've located the sheets, double check the wallboard for any late scratches. They will be identified by a squiggly line drawn through the name. Be sure and mark the late scratches on your entry sheets.

Each horse at no matter what track will have an individual number printed on the entry sheet. These numbers usually correspond with the post position the horse will be running out of. For example, let's say there's 12 horses running in the 6th race at Hollywood Park. The entry sheet will be printed somewhat like the following:

HOLLYWOOD PARK

Track Conditions Fast

6th Race

1 1/16 miles 3yo & up Claiming

801	JOHN JAMES	5/2	Baze	118
802	MISS MUSTARD	6	Pincay	116
803	SIR HONOR	12	Stevens	116
804	TAP'S SISTER	30	Shoemaker	116
805	FINISHED PRODUCT	5	Toro	114
806	SO SHE GOES	10	McCarron	116
807	LAST OUT	9/2	Valenzuela	118
808	TINY MISS	2	Aragon	112
809	SHE'S PERFECT	3	Delahoussaye	118
810	FUNNY KID	4	Meza	116
811	PLASTIC SURGEON	20	Ortega	116
812	DOC'S HANDLE	50	Pedroza	116

Number 801, will be the #1 horse in the post parade and will also race out of post position #1. While number 812, will be the #12 horse and will race out of position #12. That looks simple enough doesn't it. The tricky part comes when there are horses running as an entry, and there has been a scratch or a late scratch. Let's take the same race again.

6th Race

2 801 JOHN JAMES
3 802 MISS MUSTARD
4 803 SIR HONOR
1 804 (a) TAP'S SISTER
5 805 FINISHED PRODUCT
1A 806 (a) SO SHE GOES
6 807 LAST OUT
~~**9** 808 TINY MISS~~
8 809 SHE'S PERFECT
9 810 FUNNY KID
~~**10** 811 PLASTIC SURGEON~~
11 812 DOC'S HANDLE

NOTE: The numbers in boldface to the left of the horse's betting number, is the actual number the horse will have on his saddle cloth.

TAP'S SISTER and SO SHE GOES are running as the (a) entry. Note the

"A" that's in parentheses before the horse's name. When this occurs, you should renumber your entry sheet so you can correspond the number with the horse's numbers in the post parade.

As the horses go parade to post, TAP'S SISTER will be the #1 horse, SO SHE GOES will be the #1a, JOHN JAMES will be #2, and DOC'S HANDLE will be the #10 horse. TINY MISS was a late scratch, so there will be no number 7 horse or saddle cloth in the race. PLASTIC SURGEON was an automatic scratch, so his number 10 will go to DOC'S HANDLE. At many of the race books, they will have renumbered the entry sheets, but many do not. The renumbering is very important to know, for if the #1 horse in the post parade looked muscled to the hilt and you bet on horse number 801, (thinking it was the #1 horse in the post parade,) you would be crying after the cashier told you that number 804 was the winner. It's a little confusing, but now that I've explained how it works, it's simple, right?

If you've had time to handicap *The Form* before getting to the race book, I would suggest entering your top three selections on your entry sheet with a number and a circle around it. If not, then just concentrate on the visual positives you'll see and make your selections from them.

The T.V. monitors for each track will show the track odds as they change. For those of you who bet underlays and overlays, you'll have a good chance of doing that here. Also, any late scratches will be identified periodically, as well as jockey changes and sometimes equipment changes, as they roll by on the bottom of the screen. (In New York and Pimlico, horses racing with mud caulks or stickers will be indicated, whatever the surface condition.)

Anywhere from 12 to 7 minutes prior to post time, the horses will be shown going parade to post. The lead pony often is in such a position that it's difficult to see all of the horse, but many cameras are located so you actually get a fairly good view.

Much of the visual positives that I have instructed you on will also be identifiable through the T.V. monitors, however, you will only have a matter of seconds to view each horse. When viewing the horses, concentrate on and record: the dappled coat, the arched tail, eagerness, the racing muscle, and any muscle you can see in the flank area. To do this, I normally will turn my entry sheet over and will record the number of the horse and any positives I can see as they go by. If I don't see any positives, I just record the horses number, signifying that I saw the horse but there was no positive that I could see.

Let's take a sprint race first. The age level is 3 & up males and they're going 6 furlongs. If the cameras give good footage in the paddock you can pick up many positive signs here, such as pawing the ground, arched tails, prancing, muscle, etc. Then, as they go parade to post, reconfirm these positives and follow them as much as you can until they get to the gate. DO NOT take your eyes off the T.V. monitor, as they go parade to post, for if you do, you'll surely miss a horse passing by.

For any race of fillies and mares, 3 & up, my top priority is to find the filled out look.

For two year olds, I look for eagerness, (alert, ears pricked) but in a calm sort of way.

For horses going a route my top priority is to find a horse prancing, and muscled. I'm always looking for muscle no matter the age or distance.

After you've seen the horses, you'll have a few minutes before the race will go off. Transfer your positives to the right side of your entry sheet for that race. Remember, the more positives, the better. Don't forget to take into consideration the weight and the distance of the race. (And remember when it is time for Clydesdales and Shetland ponies.)

Once you've made your selection, take your entry sheet to the teller's window, give them the number of the horse you want to bet on, (number 804) the amount you wish to wager, ($2.00 on up, however, some race books will take a $1.00 exacta bet), and the type of bet you wish to make, (Win, Place, Exacta, Quinella, etc.) preferably in that order. Casinos have computerized their race books and will give you that type of ticket. BE SURE, after getting your ticket, that you DO NOT LEAVE THE TELLER'S WINDOW UNTIL YOU HAVE VERIFIED THAT THE NUMBER OF THE HORSE YOU WISHED TO WAGER ON HAS BEEN CORRECTLY KEYED INTO THE COMPUTER AND YOU RECEIVED THE CORRECT CHANGE. Tears have been shed by yours truly, because of incorrectly written tickets. Believe me, it happens here, just like it does at your local track.

If your horse wins the race, take your ticket to the race book cashier's window. There will only be one, and I hope to see you there.

XVI.
POWERFUL PADDOCK PLAYS

POWERFUL PADDOCK PLAYS

There are two ways to profit from the content of "Horses Talk—It Pays to Listen:" (1) as an added aspect of the horse player's basic handicapping; and (2) as a separate, and potentially very lucrative "angle play." Jim would like to make some recommendations in both areas toward maximizing your profit.

"CONVENTIONAL" HANDICAPPING

There are as many theories and approaches to Thoroughbred handicapping as there are books on the "horse racing" shelves of Gambler's Book Club in Las Vegas. In reality, most horse players open the *Daily Racing Form,* and apply, as best possible, the elements that they have gleaned from an assortment of books, magazines, seminars, and whatever other resources available.

The goal is parimutuel profit, which means betting enough winners to subsidize losing tickets, costs of being a "horse player," and some extra dollars remaining.

My first piece of advice is to remember, always, that there are two types of winning—betting winning horses, and NOT BETTING horses that lose. Every potential bet that is not made, and the horse LOSES, is a secondary addition to overall profit.

For every race that produces off analysis a "playable" horse, there are several that deliver a clear two or three horse contention, but no way to narrow to a single choice based on Speed, Pace, and the other general handicapping measurements (trainer, jockey, etc.). Based on the *Daily Racing Form* and other informational tools, the race is a "Pass" at least in terms of a Win bet.

Paddock and post parade skills will pick winners in many such races. Often, in an initial three-horse contention, one horse will stand out in this appraisal of the horses themselves. In other cases, two will look so dull and/or exhibit such negative signs that the third horse is a betting candidate off elimination of the other two.

When paddock and post parade skills and judgment of the actual "horse flesh" reinforce a betting decision, the wager can be made with a much greater "comfort zone." Once a horse player has expectations of parimutuel success, presumably he/she will adopt a wagering strategy that adjusts bet size to proficiency (the best of which is Jacada's "BB+SR"—Base Bet Plus Square Root of Profits).

The moment the horse player has a positive balance of win percentage vs average payoff—bet size increases by leaps and bounds. MANY who previously view themselves as "professional" find that a $10 bet is much different than a $400 bet in terms of the head trip that results. Psychological pressure can create mistakes, and as bet size increases, the most common is timidity.

The player will inevitably tilt toward "conservatism," betting most frequently the selections that are favored by the public, and backing off those at longer odds. This is, of course, dead wrong. Any betting target that qualifies as a "play"—AND is going off at a price—should have AT LEAST as much on him/her as would be wagered on any selection viewed as the winning contender, that happens to be a heavy favorite.

No one can exceed Trillis and I in failing to have equal commitment to longshot candidates; it is a psychological hang-up that we share with more horse players than will admit to the frailty. We find, increasingly, that when the post parade/paddock also keys the selection—it is much easier to lay bigger numbers on the Win end.

The paddock/post parade inspections and analysis are also critical in other avenues of wagering. In exacta wagering, the paddock will frequently deliver the longshot that comes first or second, and creates the boxcar payoff.

At tracks, large and small, before the first race I, would encourage the reader to turn to each exacta race on the program, and circle the name of every trainer known for high percentage results in gimmick race competition. If trainer data—in detailed break-down—is not available commercially, any serious horse player MUST build personal records—to AT LEAST know win percentages, sprint vs route, and gimmick (Exactas, Perfectas, Trifectas, Daily Double) vs non-gimmick.

In each such race, when going to the paddock, these trainers' horses will particularly get a close look. Even the Pick Six can carry a value from the study and note-taking from paddock and post parade. This occurs where the Pick Six races are being considered, and the player notes from the previous race one of the stronger body signs. As an advance bet, as with the Daily Double, the player cannot use TODAY'S visuals. But previous race notations will trigger the inclusion of a contender that otherwise might be a PASS.

Whether the Pick Six pays $3000 at Beulah Park, or builds to seven figures at a major track, take a look at those pools that go to a single ticket, often off either one or two BIG longshot winners. Usually, these single ticket winners are not the result of some form of MAGIC. If not belonging to the trainer(s) of the day's longshot(s), the person who has included said horse(s) in the Pick Six ticket has done so off previous race notations (paddock analysis, possibly combined with either previous race "trouble," or sometimes a pedigree fit to today's distance and surface.)

As stated, the first use of the skills available through this book is in fine-tuning handicapped choices via some form of conventional handicapping. It will be maximally beneficial, as one moves down the ladder of "track class."

Where attendance and parimutuel handle are lower, purse schedules are far below the costs of racing. Owners and trainers will need parimutuel profits as a supplement to purse earnings. And there will be many, many "walking wounded." There will also be more trainers who are either hobbyists or incompetents, so there will be many horses that are not properly conditioned and cared for.

But even at the most prestigious tracks, post parade and paddock analysis will produce tremendous payoffs. The reference Trillis makes to the "tight flank" I quickly learned was a dynamite body sign. The first time I saw it on television here was in the simulcasting of the California Derby. D. Wayne Lukas had vanned up PARIS PRINCE, and when he entered the track you could see three parallel "bulges" running from just behind the saddle cloth toward the rear. He was the equine equivalent of the Malibu "Muscle Beach" fraternity, a horse version of Arnold Schwartzenegger. He paid $52.

My friend, John Ball, calls them "Havana cigars"—when the horse is fully developed, it looks like someone slipped three "Havanas" under the outer skin. This was seen this year on such Stakes winners as WISE TIMES (his longshot payoff just before the Marlboro), ESTRAPADE (when winning the Arlington Million, who would have been a double-digit payoff if not having to be part of the entry with the washed out AL MAMOON, the crowd favorite), and others.

To further illustrate, I would share with all readers a multi-purpose illustration in a letter from a Seattle subscriber, received toward the end of the 1986 Longacres race meet. The first TF (tight flank, Havana cigar horse) he spotted after Trillis's June seminar was dead last in a six furlong contest. At first, it was a disappointment—until he returned home, and noticed in his file that the trainer was something like 5% at the sprint distances and 30%+ at routes. One week later the horse was back, entered at 1 1/16 mile. The "cigars" were still there; he increased his bet, and collected $58 for each $2.

Through the remainder of the season, he noted—as is common—that this body sign was not seen often. But in cashing seven additional wins, the cheapest price was over $10, a win percentage approaching 50% and average payoff over $30. This is GOOD hunting.

I cannot stress this paddock and post parade skill too much. In today's racing, there is more and more manipulation—enough to seriously taint any expectations as to consistent results from the standards like Speed and Pace. A trainer may try to fake out horse players with unnecessary leg wraps, complete with ointment discoloration, an effort to create the appearance of a seriously "walking wounded." He may dye a tongue-tie strap to be literally invisible. But there is NO WAY the trainer can hide a TF—or a deep racing muscle—or dappled skin.

ANYONE taking a little time and mastering the material in this book will take a quantum leap past 98% of racing fans competing for parimutuel payouts. Three different 1985–86 studies declared that 98% of horse players lose, 2% win. That 2% is a combination of paddock "specialists," Thoroughbred trainers and their cohorts.

THE PPP ANGLE PLAY

This is a powerful play. There are three requirements: #1—trainer performance (win percentage, sprint vs route, at some tracks this information is publicly marketed); #2—record on your program, and convert to running totals, all horses that race with a tongue-tie (I will explain why shortly); #3—paddock/post parade appraisal of the horses, and program notations per Trillis's recommendations.

To elaborate as to tongue-ties, many horses race with same and do not win. But they are running for trainers that could not win a race with SECRETARIAT—who DO NOT know how to condition and take care of a Thoroughbred. But at the tracks we have checked, there will be 20–30 trainers, whose wins with "tongue-tie horses" vs "tongue-tie starts" is several times higher than their total wins vs total starts. With any one of THESE trainers, a tongue-tie is a major signpost.

Another major signpost—in terms of equipment—is the use of "stickers" on fast tracks and turf. Generally, this turns up as a positive correlation with the very same trainers.

Either of these equipment/trainer correlations constitutes a bet if there are ANY positive body signs.

Among the positive body signs, I would cite three as solely and by themselves justifying an ANGLE PLAY wager if any ONE of them is seen. These are: (1) the tight flank—to the point that the three parallel bulges are prominent; (2) the racing muscle, PROVIDED that it is deep, runs all the way to the juncture of tail and rump; (3) at routes at 1 1/16 mile, and especially longer, a goose rump.

#1, above, you will rarely EVER see more than one in the same race. It warrants an automatic bet. If it DOES NOT win, it is important to watch for the horse to come back in its next race. ANY horse can be wiped out by adverse racing luck (or if entered in wrong Race Conditions, no trainer intentions to win). If this body sign is still present when the horse next starts, it is increasingly valid. This level of conditioning cannot be maintained indefinitely. Any competent trainer will be determined to get a win payoff before the horse goes off form.

#2—if there are two horses in the race shod with stickers (fast track or turf,) and both have a positive trainer correlation, "dutch" the two (bet both). If there are three such horses, trainer-qualified, toss the lowest odds, and "dutch" the other two. If there are four or more horses thus shod and qualified, reduce this signpost to the second tier (covered further, shortly).

#3—same ground rules as #2. In major Stakes, which are substantially at the more classic distances, up to half the field will have goose rumps, and it becomes simply a positive body sign. But outside Stakes competition, especially as we have viewed the East Coast, it is not uncommon to see claiming routes where only one entry has this conformation. Wins and payoffs to 25–1 have been consistent.

In addition to the above, there is a fourth "play" qualification—a horse is a bet if it shows any FIVE of the second-tier signposts. These are defined as:

(1) Tongue-tie, trainer correlation not yet established
(2) Stickers (fast track or turf), trainer correlation not yet established
(3) Dappling
(4) Shiny coat (the kind that blinds)
(5) Racing muscle, deep but not all the way to the rump
(6) Alert and well-groomed
(7) Goose rump (routes only)
(8) Turf races—big hooves
(9) Off-track conditions—either the largest or smallest horse in the race ("Clydesdale" or "Shetland pony")
(10) Arched tail
(11) Eagerness signs
(12) Fillies—fullness of flank and stomach (not underweight)

Obviously, qualification for a bet implies an absence of negative body signs. If the horse shows discolored kidney sweat or scraggly coat (bad case of worms), dull coat, listless and disinterested attitude—then PASS.

There are two other potential qualifiers for this Angle Play. Neither really fits with the above. If a horse's ears are "frozen," indicating he/she has been drugged with an "upper," there are two scenarios. The horse will very likely either win the race or break down.

If the price on the horse is chalky, I would PASS the race. If the horse is over 5–1, I would bet, as the win price will balance for the horses that wind up destroyed. If the horse is 10–1 or better, the player should also consider it as a "key horse" in exacta or Trifecta investment.

During the past year, where it has been possible to log in results, the winning percentage vs average payoff has been high, where there is a correlation of a tongue-tie and the horse running on Lasix. I would NOT play into this correlation at low odds, or IF the horse is definitely a KNOWN bleeder. (If the horse has run a number of races on Lasix, probably with and without a tongue-tie, forget it—I would eliminate any horse LEGITIMATELY on Lasix after its second start on the drug).

But BECAUSE Lasix can mask so many illegal substances, converting them by race testing to metabolytes that are not interpreted by the Rules of Racing as "unlawful substances," the tongue-tie—combined with the horse being on Lasix for the first or second time—is a worthwhile risk, proportional to how much the odds exceed 5–1.

If you use the contents of this book to follow the PPP Angle Play, hopefully you will use BB+SR wagering strategy. If you are not familiar with this approach to wagering, simply send us a self-addressed, stamped envelope, and we will forward explanation and illustration.

I am sure that Trillis will appreciate hearing from readers, as to their experiences in applying paddock and post parade skills, as well as those who would be interested in a "live" seminar or personal tutoring.

Finally, once you have honed these skills at the track(s) of your choice, you may wish to test yourself against the multi-track simulcasts of the ever-expanding Las Vegas Race Books (but I would not recommend Nevada in spite of its many enticements UNTIL the reader has a solid comfort zone as to proficiency, based on at-the-track application).

Per my "introduction" premise, ANYONE can master these skills, but the "dues" will be many trips to the paddock until and as the learning process continues—and this learning process NEVER ends. Thoroughbred racing is ever changing, both individual tracks and as an industry. So the player faces constant challenge—that's part of the fun of it, and keeping pace is what PRESERVES your EDGE.

—James N. Selvidge

XVII.
MORE HORSES TALK

MORE HORSES TALK

On December 22, 1986, the printing of 500 copies of "Horses Talk: It Pays To Listen" was completed. As I pledged in those books, if there was additional material that needed to be shared, I would make sure all 500 previous purchasers would receive it as long as I had their names and addresses.

In March of 1987, the 500 copies were sold out, and orders were still coming in. I decided to self-publish more copies, and add to it additional material which would be of value to you.

First off, I owe a "thank you" to Howard Schwartz of Gambler's Book Club, and also to a long time acquaintance, Stephen States, for their assistance in catching the undetected typos in the first edition. No matter how many times I had it proofread, I was still finding more. Hopefully, we have these corrected now.

For anyone having one of the first 500 copies, please change the zip code on the copyright page to 89170 instead of 89102. I would hate to have you write to me and I not get it.

Let's start first with a few letters I've received that have very valid questions.

Dear Trillis,

"Thank you for your informative book, but I need help! I have been to Santa Anita four times, all on weekends or holidays. I must have seen approximately 320 horses, (9 per race x 9 races = 81 x 4). Here is what I perceived."

1—"Stickers on the turf is almost a sure thing."
2—"There seems to be no significance of the following signs: arched tails, dapples, nice shine."
3—"I did not notice the following: PAW, T, FO, YYY, BET."
4—"I have a problem noticing a goose rump."
5—"I have not seen one horse with HAVANA CIGARS. Is this possible? When the horses gallop from the post parade, I think I see them but then it seems that most do."

"I know my inexperience accounts for a lot of these LACK OF OBSERVATIONS but what advice can you give?"

Sincerely,
M. W.—San Pedro, CA.

Answer:

Dear M. W.,

I am happy to hear that you agree about stickers on the turf. As you say, "almost a sure thing."

As you've only been able to attend the track on weekends and holidays, and at Santa Anita (America's #1 track), you have been viewing horses that are the "cream of the crop." Many horses will be dappled, show nice shines with arched tails, and will display deep racing muscles. What you need to do on these days, (weekends or holidays) is watch for any single horse that has all these positive signs. I'm surprised you didn't notice any horse on it's toes. "T"—Usually many prance around on their toes. This is truly a positive if noticed in the walking ring and he remains that way through the parade to post.

The PAW, FO, YYY, and BET conditions are not seen on a regular basis. Maybe one out of every 400 horses watched at your big apple tracks. It's important to be aware of it though when you do see it, for it's truly a positive betting angle when spotted.

Only concern yourself with the goose rump on route races. The rear of the horse looks as though it's chopped off. You'll see it with more practice.

Yes, it is possible that you haven't seen the Havana Cigars yet. Don't strain your eyes too much to see these. Just glance quickly in the flank area—if they are there, they will bounce right out at you, (figuratively speaking).

I would suggest trying to get to the track on a weekday if at all possible. There is an entirely different crop racing then. Also, if you could attend a different track other than Santa Anita, you'll see fewer positives, and those that have them, will really stand out. Other tracks don't seem to run or have stabled the "cream of the crop" like Santa Anita does.

You're off to a good start. Take your time and it will all come together.

Best Regards,
Trillis

Dear Trillis,

"In your book you mentioned how you look for Tootsie Rolls in the flank area of the horse. On page 12 you give an illustration of the horses conformation. In the flank area I looked for some indicator of Tootsie Rolls but could see nothing. Where, during paddock inspection, does one look for these? Please give me an illustration."

Sincerely,
P. K.—Palm Beach, FL.

Answer:

Dear P. K.,

Watch for the Tootsie Rolls while in the walking ring. If you spot them while walking, this indicates the more muscled horse. I also try to make sure they appear on both sides of the horse. I have wagered on them, only appearing on one side, and have lost. If spotted while walking, and they're on both sides, and the horse still doesn't win, I would only guess the horse is either at his/her wrong distance or maybe "ouchie" because of too much muscle. Often this occurs with the superior athlete.

I have included page 12 and marked horizontal lines in the flank area where the Tootsie Rolls will be visible.

Please note, I've also marked in the Racing Muscle and will include both on the rewrite original. Many thanks for the idea.

Best regards,
Trillis

I'd like to insert here that when we speak of Tootsie Rolls, or Havana Cigars, we are also referring to "Tight Flanks." They are all the same thing.

Dear Trillis,

"I would like to share with you an interesting observation I encountered last fall at Longacres."

"My friend and I were at the paddock watching some maiden two year olds who were entered in the 4th race on Monday, October 13th, at the distance of one mile. My friend pointed out BREWSTER REWSTER because of his unusual name. As we looked at the horse, his lips were shaking like a vibrator; his mouthpiece was clicking; and his bridle was shaking. I looked into the horse's eyes and told my friend, "this horse is scared s—-less! He would rather be under a tree eating his oats." It was BREWSTER REWSTER'S 6th start of his career in which his best finish was 4th by 5 1/2 lengths. Even though he was trembling so, he finished 9th of 10 by 26 lengths and on the way back to the barn the horse collapsed and died. The next day the paper confirmed he died of a heart attack. I was not really surprised. It

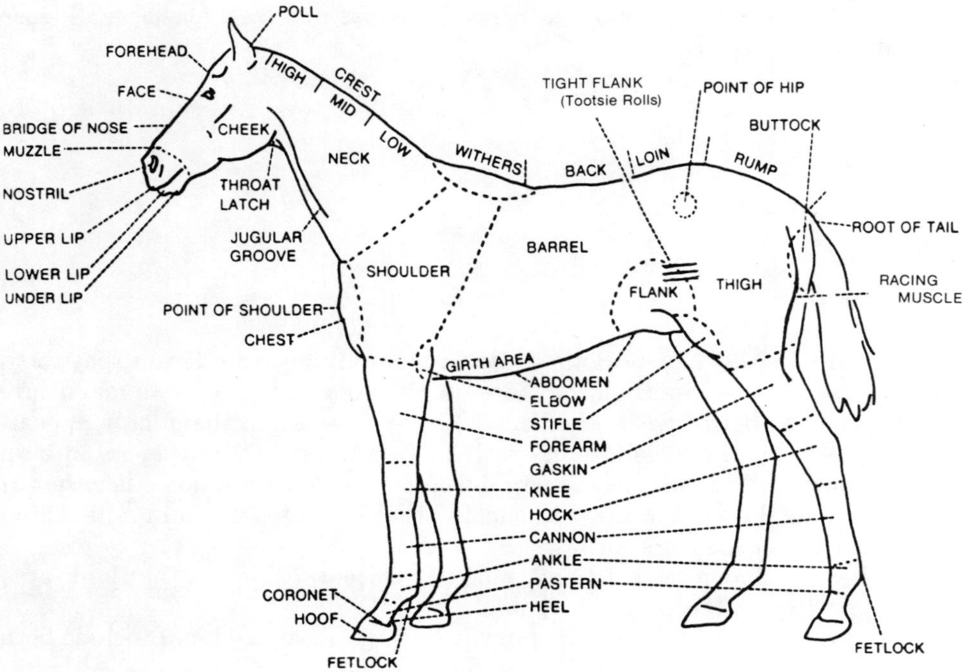

was no fluke; I had spotted the negatives, and the worst had happened. I really felt sorry for that horse. I could just tell he didn't want to be a race horse. The signals were that strong. I'll never forget that look in his eyes. I've observed the shaky lips a few other times. I've added this to your list of negative signposts."

Sincerely,
J. H.
Mercer Island, WA.

Answer:

Dear J. H.

Thanks so much for your letter. You have brought to my attention one of the negatives that I was afraid I'd forget to discuss when writing my book.

Any horse that is shaking or trembling as you say BREWSTER REWSTER was, should not be raced. He was either sick, poorly schooled or drugged.

Fright may cause a horse to tremble, but only for a short period of time. An unfamiliar object could cause a horse to tremble, but most of the time the horse will act up by rearing and kicking when this occurs. If this occurs the handler is usually able to calm the horse down once the unfamiliar object has been removed.

Before BREWSTER REWSTER was raced he had to pass the inspection of the Identifier, Paddock Judge, Track Veterinarian and the Starting Judge, and still the horse was not scratched from the race. As far as I'm concerned this is "cruelty to animals," and like I've stated before, "the officials, are blind in one eye and can't see out of the other."

Sometimes, when horses are drugged, there are side effects, and what they are feeling terrifies them. An overdose of some drugs being used can cause the heart to fail. Unfortunately, in these cases an autopsy is rarely performed, and whatever the cause, the public will never be told.

Let's hope BREWSTER REWSTER is Horse Heaven's Derby winner for 1987.

Best regards,
Trillis

J. M. From Dallas, TX., sent in a news article from The Dallas Morning News, that I feel needs to be shared. The article was printed on January 18, 1987, and titled "The Electric Horsemen."

The article tells the story of a former jockey who packed or used a machine, (buzzer) on more than 1000 mounts in his 20 year career. He tells how the machine is powered by AA batteries with two live prongs at the bottom that shock the horse when poked in the neck.

The picture below to the left shows what a machine or buzzer actually looks like and the one to the right is a diagram of one.

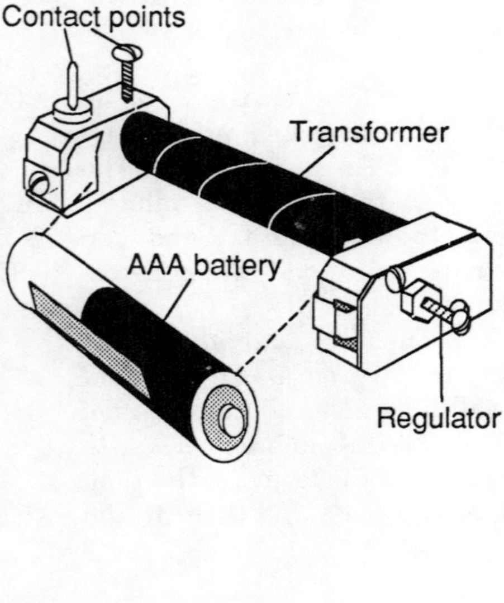

The machine is usually used in short bursts during the beginning and end of a race. It can be hidden in the waistband of the jockeys athletic supporter, or behind several pairs of goggles in his helmet, or under the elastic hem at the bottom of his pants leg. Some will tie them neatly inside the knot that they use to shorten the excess rein, and others carry a whip with a machine built into the handle.

Jockeys often are asked to carry machines by trainers and will fake packing one in order to secure mounts. As this jockey says, "At some tracks, if you don't use a machine, you don't ride." Naturally if caught the jockey gets the blame, not the trainer.

It just doesn't seem fair that a trainer can inject illegal drugs into a horse and may only get fined or suspended for a couple of months, while a jockey caught with a machine usually gets suspended for 2 years to life. Either case constitutes "cruelty to animals" and you know who is against that. On the other hand, jockeys have been known to flash machines to large bettors to secure free bets for themselves. Some test the horse in races or morning workouts to gauge their response. If the response is sufficient, they'll bet on the horse and use the machine in the race.

Machines can cause a horse to sulk and quit trying. They only improve the performance of about 10% and only help the lazy or exceptionally smart. A horse has no defense against a machine. "It's not the shock, but the sense of surprise that makes them run."

The article was excellent. I wish I could print it entirely. Just remember, if you've been told there's no such thing as a "buzzer" or "machine" in racing, then I'm afraid the person that told you obviously has never been to a race, has a few screws loose, or prefers to hide the truth.

Many thanks to J. M., for sending in the article. Here's hoping that the R.A.S.C.A.L. Association can start fighting some of these problems and clean up the sport we love so well.

E. W. From Dallas, Texas, has come up with an excellent method of refreshing his memory of all the positive and negative signposts to watch for while at the track.

The form on the right he designed and had printed up on stick-on paper. When he goes to the track he adheres one to his program and can easily refer to it when necessary.

The form is divided into 3 groups; program, paddock/walking ring, and post parade. The capital abbreviations to the left of the form are the positive signposts and those to the

POS.		NEG.
	·············PROGRAM·············	
BL	— BUTE AND LASIX	
L	— LASIX	
MC	— MUD CAULKS	
	······PADDOCK/WALKING RING······	
AT	— ARCHED TAIL	
BH	— BIG HORSE	
	BULGING LEG BANDS ····	(BLB)
CM	— CONDITIONING MUSCLE	
C	— CALM	

right are the negative. The abbreviations in brackets on the right side are identifiers E. W. has added himself which is great. E. W. has kindly given me permission to print his form and if you feel it would help you too, please feel free to copy it.

Thanks E. W., you're a jewel and a genius.

DAP—	DAPPLED COAT	
FO —	FILLED OUT FILLY	
	FILLY-PATCH	(FP)
	FRIGHTENED-FRACTIOUS	F
GR —	GOOSE RUMP (ROUTES)	
	KIDNEY SWEAT-LEGS	KS
	MOUTH GREEN FOAM	(MG)
NS —	NICE SHINE	
PAW—	PAWING THE GROUND	
RM —	RACING MUSCLE	
S —	STICKERS (TURF)	
SH —	SMALL HORSE (OFF TRK.—RT.)	
	SUNKEN-DRAWN IN FLANK	(SDF)
T —	ON TOES—W.R-P.P.	
TF —	TIGHT FLANK	
TT —	TONGUE TIE	
	WASHY-SWEATING	W
	POST PARADE	
BET—	NOSE TO NECK OF L.P.	
	QUICK SHORT STEPS	(Q)
RC —	REAR HOOVES CLOSE	
YYY—	YES, YES, YES	

MORE ON OFF TRACKS

When the weather turns bad and the track becomes sloppy, the handicapper encounters additional problems as well as the adverse weather conditions.

1—One must try to figure how intent the trainer is on winning.

Any trainer who takes the time to tie the horses tail up so mud and added weight will be limited, surely has a greater win intent in mind then one that doesn't. The same holds true with a trainer that spends money to put mud caulks on vs one that doesn't.

2—One must determine the attitude of the horse towards the off track surface.

If a horse still tries to arch his tail in spite of the discomfort of the wrap, it's a very positive sign and one should absolutely ignore the tote board if this condition exists. (A signpost to longshots).

On the other hand, as the horse goes parade to post, if he looks like he's prancing on his toes when the track is muddy & sloppy, to me this is a negative signpost. He is trying to pull his hoofs off the track as quickly as possible because he doesn't like the surface condition. I look more for a horse who has a nice arched wrapped tail, and moves through the slop as if nothing bothers him.

CAPOTE in the Wood Memorial was one horse you could easily tell did not like the surface conditions. He was quickly pulling his hooves up off the surface as he was going parade to post. GULCH, on the other hand, didn't display any dislike at all.

"ATTITUDE & SPIRIT"

Countless times a horse player sees a horse make a run at the leader in the stretch, but can't or won't pass the other horse. In the *Daily Racing Form* result charts, it usually says the horse "hung in the stretch."

Why does this happen so often, when we also see a smaller group of others that whistle right on by?

At other times, we see two horses race head and head in most of the race, and then they cave in and everyone else goes by them both in the stretch. But then other times, the two front-runners continue their duel right down to the wire, leaving the rest of the field far behind.

Sometimes these differences are explained by the difference in the track surface, good or bad for front speed vs closers. But as in everything else about racing, it is wrong to generalize. If we can continue to learn, we can get better and better about matching the right answer to the right question.

A horse's "spirit" will get a lot of argument from some, who will claim this is something that can't be inherited. That may be. But a horse tends to behave based on what he has learned, and it is important to understand that.

If you could spend some time at breeding farms, you would quickly see that the horse's first teacher is his mother. This is the beginning of what they call "pecking order." An aggressive mother will shove the other mares aside and be first to the water with her baby by her side. She will be first to the feed bin. And she will be teaching her baby to be "first."

Commonly, there will be one or two other mares that give in to #1, but will edge out the rest. Their children will not have as big a dose of being first, but they will learn "trying." They will not be content to be behind everybody else.

Those mares, and their babies, who yield, and let themselves get pushed to the rear of the food/water crowding, will not have a foundation of aggressive behavior when they start training for races.

If we could somehow know what names are given to all those that are not only first, but trying, we could watch for them to hit the track, see who is their trainer, and we would have a big EDGE.

This is not possible, so we must remember that the next best thing is to learn to "read" signposts of "attitude" and "spirit," as well as physical conditioning.

After a Thoroughbred is barely a year old, it may go through a Yearling Sale, or into training for a breeder/owner. In either event, it must be "broken." This is a very important time. The more spirited a horse is the harder to "break." Sadly, some handlers, who are not the best, BREAK the spirit in the process.

This "breaking process" is usually followed by a month or two off before the horse is put into training at the track. Who has the horse in this period, and how the horse is handled, also has much to do with the attitude the horse may carry the rest of his/her life.

Finally, once racing as a two year old, the horse has a trainer, who has grooms and assistants. This is kind of like a small boy's first experience with school and teachers, the principal, and other kids. If the horse is well taken care of, it can wind up a winning horse for many years, barring injury. But if the horse is treated badly, or has really bad experiences, it may be psychologically scarred for life. A mishandled horse in the paddock/walking ring will not have the attitude or spirit of a winner.

As an example, I recently watched a race for young horses; Angel Cordero, Jr. was on the favorite. Cordero is a great jockey, but by the luck of the race his horse was second. After passing the finish line, once he stood up in the saddle, he hit the horse with his whip, then much to my surprise he actually hit him again. I mean come on guys, is this what you do when you're a poor loser?

That horse from now on will recognize Cordero as he mounts and will remember that even though he races as hard and as fast as he can he'll still get punished when he crosses the finish line. This horse who may have had some "spirit" may now have an "attitude" problem toward Cordero. If I were the horse, I'd buck him right off the next time he mounted. If I were the trainer, I'd say thanks, but no thanks, we won't be needing your services anymore. Wonderfully enough, the trainer did just that, and this young horse went on to win the 1987 Wood Memorial with a jockey on his back that cared. The "spirit" and "attitude" of this horse could have been completely destroyed if changes were not made.

We will see in the *Daily Racing Form* many horses with bad running lines, rarely winning a race. Where it is a matter of "talent," dropping the horse may make it more competitive. But if the running lines result from attitude and lack of spirit, the horse may never find a winning level.

Scientists say there is no "gene" for racing courage. Many claim the horse is among the dumbest of animals. Those saying this, should watch ALYSHEBA'S stretch run in the 1987 Kentucky Derby over and over. ALYSHEBA showed fantastic courage, and was obviously taught to be first no matter what.

"Special" human beings are recognized by their I.Q., vocabulary, and accomplishments. Horses can talk to us only through their bodies. They are not all alike, so we must learn the signposts to know which are superior and which are inferior.

You've heard the saying, "the third time is the charm," and "seeing is believing." I had to find out for sure My better-half and I took two days off and drove to Furnace Creek Ranch in Death Valley, California. I was determined to ride my third horse without falling off. I am happy to announce that I am now a seasoned rider. They did however have to peel my legs off the saddle after returning from a two hour ride. It's amazing how the blood just doesn't seem to circulate for a few minutes after you've gotten off a horse.

Wishing you the very best of racing seasons.

Best Regards,
Trillis